Allyn and Bacon

Sociology on the Net
2001 Edition

Joe Jacoby
Bowling Green University

Doug Gotthoffer
California State University–Northridge

D1401999

Allyn and Bacon
Boston • London • Toronto • Sydney • Tokyo • Singapore

Series Editor: Jeff Lasser
Multimedia Editor: Nina Tisch
Editorial Production: Marla Feuerstein
Cover Creative Director: Kate Conway
Cover Designer: Amy Braddock
Editorial Production Service: Omegatype Typography, Inc.

NOTICE: Between the time Web site information is gathered and then published, it is not unusual for some sites to have ceased operating. Also, the transcription of URLs can result in unintended typographical errors. The Publisher would appreciate notification where these occcur so that they may be corrected in subsequent editions. Thank you.

In its effort to provide a diverse list of Web sites, the Publisher has included links that do not necessarily represent the views of Allyn and Bacon. Faculty, students, and researchers are strongly advised to use their analytical skills to determine the truth, accuracy, and value of the content in individual Web sites.

TRADEMARK CREDITS: Where information was available, trademarks and registered trademarks are indicated below. When detailed information was not available, the publisher has indicated trademark status with an initial capital where those names appear in the text.

Macintosh is a registered trademark of Apple Computer, Inc.

Microsoft is a registered trademark of Microsoft Corporation. Windows, Windows95, and Microsoft Internet Explorer are trademarks of Microsoft Corporation.

Netscape and the Netscape Navigator logo are registered trademarks of Netscape Communications Corporation.

Copyright © 2001 by Allyn and Bacon
A Pearson Education Company
Needham Heights, Massachusetts 02494
Internet: www.abacon.com

ISBN 0-205-32798-2

Printed in the United States of America

10   9   8   7   6   5   4   3   2   1   03   02   01   00

Contents

Introduction to the Internet

You're about to embark on an exciting experience as you become one of the millions of citizens of the Internet. Once you've accustomed yourself to this wonderful new world, you'll be amazed by how much you can discover, learn, and accomplish as you explore the Internet's dynamic resources.

Some Things You Ought to Know

Much of the confusion over the Internet comes from two sources. One is terminology. Just as the career you're preparing for has its own special vocabulary, so does the Internet. You'd be hard pressed to join in the shoptalk of archeologists, librarians, or carpenters if you didn't speak their language. Don't expect to plop yourself down in the middle of the Internet without some buzzwords under your belt, either.

The second source of confusion is that there are often many ways to accomplish the same ends on the Internet. This is a direct by-product of the freedom so highly cherished by Net citizens. When someone has an idea for doing something, he or she puts it out there and lets the Internet community decide its merits. As a result, it's difficult to put down in writing the *one exact* way to send email or find information on slugs or whatever.

In addition, there are differences in the workings of a PC or Mac and the various versions of the two major browsers, Netscape Communicator (or Navigator) and Internet Explorer. If you can't find a particular command or function mentioned in the book on your computer, chances are it's there, but in a different place or with a slightly different name. Check the manual or online help that came with your computer, or ask a more computer-savvy friend or professor.

And relax. Getting up to speed on the Internet takes a little time, but the effort will be well rewarded. Approach learning your way around the Internet with the same enthusiasm and curiosity you approach learning your way around a new college campus. This isn't a competition. Nobody's keeping score. And the only winner will be you.

In *Understanding Media,* Marshall McLuhan presaged the existence of the Internet when he described electronic media as an extension of our central nervous system. On the other hand, today's students introduced to the Internet for the first time describe it as "Way cool."

No matter which description you favor, you are immersed in a period in our culture that is transforming the way we live by transforming the nature of the information we live by. As recently as 1980, intelligence was marked by "knowing things." If you were born in that year, by the time you were old enough to cross the street by yourself, that definition had changed radically. Today, in a revolution that makes McLuhan's vision tangible, events, facts, rumors, and gossip are distributed instantly to all parts of the global body. The effects are equivalent to a shot of electronic adrenaline. No longer the domain of the privileged few, information is shared by all the inhabitants of McLuhan's global village. Meanwhile, the concept of information as intelligence feels as archaic as a television remote control with a wire on it (ask your parents about that).

With hardly more effort than it takes to rub your eyes open in the morning you can connect with the latest news, with gossip about your favorite music group or TV star, with the best places to eat on spring break, with the weather back home, or with the trials and tribulations of that soap opera character whose life conflicts with your history class.

You can not only carry on a real-time conversation with your best friend at a college half a continent away, but you can see and hear her, too. Or, you can play interactive games with a dozen or more worldwide, world-class, challengers; and that's just for fun.

When it comes to your education, the Internet has shifted the focus from amassing information to putting that information to use. Newspaper and magazine archives are now almost instantly available, as are the contents of many reference books. Distant and seemingly unapproachable experts are found answering questions in discussion groups or in electronic newsletters.

The Internet also addresses the major problem facing all of us in our split-second, efficiency-rated culture: Where do we find the time? The

part

1

Internet allows professors and students to keep in touch, to collaborate and learn, without placing unreasonable demands on individual schedules. Professors are posting everything from course syllabi to homework solutions on the Internet, and are increasingly answering questions on-line, all in an effort to ease the pressure for face-to-face meetings by supplementing them with cyberspace offices. The Internet enables students and professors to expand office hours into a twenty-four-hour-a-day, seven-day-a-week operation. Many classes have individual sites at which enrolled students can gather electronically to swap theories, ideas, resources, gripes, and triumphs.

By freeing us from some of the more mundane operations of information gathering, and by sharpening our information-gathering skills in other areas, the Internet encourages us to be more creative and imaginative. Instead of devoting most of our time to gathering information and precious little to analyzing and synthesizing it, the Internet tips the balance in favor of the skills that separate us from silicon chips. Other Internet citizens can gain the same advantage, however, and as much as the Internet ties us together, it simultaneously emphasizes our individual skills—our ability to connect information in new, meaningful, and exciting ways. Rarely have we had the opportunity to make connections and observations on such a wide range of topics, to create more individual belief systems, and to chart a path through learning that makes information personally useful and meaningful.

part

1

A Brief History of the Internet

The 20th century's greatest advance in personal communication and freedom of expression began as a tool for national defense. In the mid-1960s, the Department of Defense was searching for an information analogy to the new Interstate Highway System, a way to move computations and computing resources around the country in the event the Cold War caught fire. The immediate predicament, however, had to do with the Defense Department's budget, and the millions of dollars spent on computer research at universities and think tanks. Much of these millions was spent on acquiring, building, or modifying large computer systems to meet the demands of the emerging fields of computer graphics, artificial intelligence, and multiprocessing (where one computer was shared among dozens of different tasks).

While the research was distributed across the country, the unwieldy, often temperamental, computers were not. This made it difficult for computer scientists at various institutions to share their computer work without duplicating each other's hardware. Wary of being accused of reinventing the wheel, the Advanced Research Projects Agency (ARPA), the funding arm of the Defense Department, invested in the ARPANET, a private network that would allow disparate computer systems to communicate with each other. Researchers could remain ensconced among their colleagues at their home campuses while using computing resources at government research sites thousands of miles away.

A small cadre of ARPANET citizens soon began writing computer programs to perform little tasks across the Internet. Most of these programs, while ostensibly meeting immediate research needs, were written for the challenge of writing them. These programmers, for example, created the first email systems. They also created games like Space Wars and Adventure. Driven in large part by the novelty and practicality of email, businesses and institutions accepting government research funds begged and borrowed their way onto the ARPANET, and the number of connections swelled.

As the innocence of the 1960s gave way the business sense of the 1980s, the government eased out of the networking business, turning the ARPANET (now Internet) over to its users. While we capitalize the word "Internet", it may surprise you to learn there is no "Internet, Inc.," no business in charge of this uniquely postmodern creation. Administration of this world-wide communication complex is still handled by the cooperating institutions and regional networks that comprise the Internet. The word "Internet" denotes a specific interconnected network of networks, and not a corporate entity.

Using the World Wide Web for Research

Just as no one owns the worldwide communication complex that is the Internet, there is no formal organization among the collection of hundreds of thousands of computers that make up the part of the Net called the World Wide Web.

If you've never seriously used the Web, you are about to take your first steps on what can only be described as an incredible journey. Initially, though, you might find it convenient to think of the Web as a giant television network with millions of channels. It's safe to say that, among all these channels, there's something for you to watch. Only, how to find it? You could click through the channels one by one, of course, but by the time you found something of interest it would (1) be over or (2) leave you wondering if there wasn't something better on that you're missing.

A more efficient way to search for what you want would be to consult some sort of TV listing. While you could skim through pages more rapidly than channels, the task would still be daunting. A more creative approach would allow you to press a button on your remote control that would connect you to a channel of interest; what's more, that channel would contain the names (or numbers) of other channels with similar programs. Those channels in turn would contain information about other channels. Now you could zip through this million-channel universe, touching down only at programs of potential interest. This seems far more effective than the hunt-and-peck method of the traditional couch potato.

If you have a feel for how this might work for television, you have a feel for what it's like to journey around (or surf) the Web. Instead of channels on the Web, we have *Web sites*. Each site contains one or more *pages*. Each page may contain, among other things, links to other pages, either in the same site or in other sites, anywhere in the world. These other pages may elaborate on the information you're looking at or may direct you to related but not identical information, or even provide contrasting or contradictory points of view; and, of course, these pages could have links of their own.

Web sites are maintained by businesses, institutions, affinity groups, professional organizations, government departments, and ordinary people anxious to express opinions, share information, sell products, or provide services. Because these Web sites are stored electronically, updating them is more convenient and practical than updating printed media. That makes Web sites far more dynamic than other types of research material you may be used to, and it means a visit to a Web site can open up new opportunities that weren't available as recently as a few hours ago.

Hypertext and Links

The invention that unveils these revolutionary possibilities is called *hypertext*. Hypertext is a technology for combining text, graphics, sounds, video, and links on a single World Wide Web page. Click on a link and you're transported, like Alice falling down the rabbit hole, to a new page, a new address, a new environment for research and communication.

Links come in three flavors: text, picture, and hot spot. A text link may be a letter, a word, a phrase, a sentence, or any contiguous combination of text characters. You can identify text links at a glance because the characters are <u>underlined</u>, and are often displayed in a unique color, setting the link apart from the rest of the text on the page. Picture links

part

1

Text
Link

Picture
Link

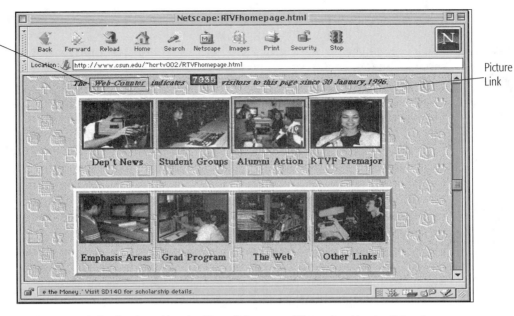

Text links are underlined and set of in color. Picture links are set off by a colored border. Hot spots carry no visual identification.

are pictures or other graphic elements. On the Web, a picture may not only be worth a thousand words, but it may also be the start of a journey into a whole new corner of cyberspace.

The third kind of link, the hot spot, is neither underlined nor bordered, a combination which would make it impossible to spot, were it not for a Web convention that offers you a helping hand finding all types of links. This helping hand is, well, a hand. Whenever the mouse cursor passes over a link, the cursor changes from an arrow to a hand. Wherever you see the hand icon, you can click and retrieve another Web page. Sweep the cursor over an area of interest, see the hand, follow the link, and you're surfing the Web.

In the Name of the Page

Zipping around the Web in this way may seem exciting, even serendipitous, but it's also fraught with perils. How, for instance, do you revisit a page of particular interest? Or share a page with a classmate? Or cite a page as a reference for a professor? Web page designers assign names, or titles, to their pages; unfortunately, there's nothing to prevent two designers from assigning the same title to different pages.

An instrument that uniquely identifies Web pages does exist. It's called a Universal Resource Locator (URL), the cyber-signposts of the World Wide Web. URLs contain all the information necessary to locate:

- the page containing the information you're looking for;
- the computer that hosts (stores) that page of information;
- the form the information is stored in.

A typical URL looks like this:

```
http://www.abacon.com/index.html
```

You enter it into the **Location** or **Address** field at the top of your browser window. Hit the **Return** (or **Enter**) key and your browser will deliver to your screen the exact page specified. When you click on a link, you're actually using a shorthand alternative to typing the URL yourself because the browser does it for you. In fact, if you watch the "Location" or "Address" field when you click on a link, you'll see its contents change to the URL you're traveling to.

part

1

The URL Exposed

How does your browser—or the whole World Wide Web structure, for that matter—know where you're going? As arcane as the URL appears, there is a logical explanation to its apparent madness. (This is true not only of URLs but also of your computer experience in general. Because a computer's "intelligence" only extends to following simple instructions exactly, most of the commands, instructions, and procedures you'll encounter have simple underlying patterns. Once you familiarize yourself with these patterns, you'll find you're able to make major leaps in your understanding of new Internet features.)

To unscramble the mysteries of World Wide Web addresses, we'll start at the end of the URL and work our way toward the front.

```
/index.html
```

This is the name of a single file or document. Eventually, the contents of this file/document will be transferred over the Internet to your computer.

However, because there are undoubtedly thousands of files on the Internet with this name, we need to clarify our intentions a bit more.

```
www.abacon.com
```

This is the name of a particular Internet *Web server,* a computer whose job it is to forward Web pages to you on request. By Internet convention, this name is unique. The combination of

```
www.abacon.com/index.html
```

identifies a unique file/document on a unique Web server on the World Wide Web. No other file has this combined address, so there's no question about which file/document to transfer to you.

The characters *http://* at the beginning of the URL identify the method by which the file/document will be transferred. The letters stand for HyperText Transfer Protocol.

part

1

Quick Check

Don't Be Lost In (Hyper)Space

Let's pause for a quick check of your Web navigation skills. Look at the sample web page on the next page. How many links does it contain?

Did you find four? The four links include:

1. The word "links" in the second line below the seaside picture;

2. The sentence "What about me?";

3. The word "cyberspace" in the quick brown fox sentence;

4. The hot spot in the seaside picture. We know there's at least one link in the picture, because the cursor appears as a hand. (There may be more hot spots on the page, but we can't tell from this picture alone.)

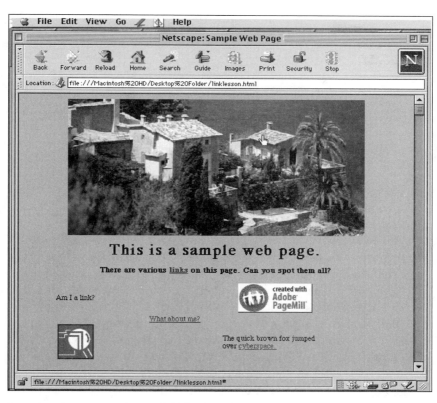

A sample web page to exercise your link identifying skills.

Getting There from Here

Now you know that a URL uniquely identifies a page and that links used as shorthand for URLs enable you to travel from page to page in the Web; but what if a link takes you someplace you don't want to go? Missing page messages take several forms, such as URL 404, Object not on this server, Missing Object, Page not Found, but they all lead to the same place—a dead end. The page specified by the link or URL no longer exists. There are many reasons for missing pages. You may have entered the URL incorrectly. Every character must be precise and no spaces are allowed. More than likely, though, especially if you arrived here via a link, the page you're after has been moved or removed. Remember, anybody can create a link to any page. In the spirit of the Internet, there are no forms to fill out, no procedures to follow. That's the good news. The bad news is that the owner of a page is under no

part

1

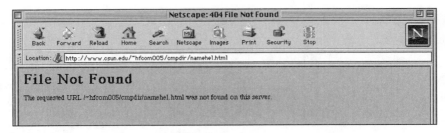

A missing page message, an all too common road hazard on the information superhighway.

obligation to inform the owners of links pointing to it that the page location has changed. In fact, there's no way for the page owner to even know about all the links to her page. Yes, the Internet's spirit of independence proves frustrating sometimes, but you'll find these small inconveniences are a cheap price to pay for the benefits you receive. Philosophy aside, though, we're still stuck on a page of no interest to us. The best strategy is to back up and try another approach.

Every time you click on the **Back** button, you return to the previous page you visited. That's because your browser keeps track of the pages you visit and the order in which you visit them. The **Back** icon, and its counterpart, the **Forward** icon, allow you to retrace the steps, forward and backward, of your cyberpath. Sometimes you may want to move two, three, or a dozen pages at once. Although you can click the **Back** or **Forward** icons multiple times, Web browsers offer an easier navigation shortcut. If you use Netscape, clicking on the **Go** menu in the menu bar displays a list of your most recently visited pages, in the order you've been there. Unlike the **Back** or **Forward** icons, you can select any page from the menu, and a single click takes you directly there. There's no need to laboriously move one page a time. If you use Internet Explorer, you can click on the **History** button in the Explorer bar to see a list of links you visited in previous days and weeks, or press the arrow at the end of the Address bar to see previously visited links.

Quick Check

As a quick review, here's what we know about navigating the Web so far:

- Enter a URL directly into the Location field;
- Click on a link;
- Use the **Back** or **Forward** icons;
- Select a page from the **Go** menu.

You Can Go Home (and to Other Pages) Again

How do we return to a page hours, days, or even months later? One way is to write down the URLs of every page we may want to revisit. There's got to be a better way, and there is: We call them bookmarks (on Netscape Communicator) or favorites (on Microsoft Internet Explorer).

Like their print book namesakes, Web bookmarks (and favorites) flag specific Web pages. Selecting an item from the **Bookmark/Favorites** menu, like selecting an item from the **Go** menu, is the equivalent of entering a URL into the **Location** field of your browser, except that items in the **Bookmark/Favorites** menu are ones you've added yourself and represent pages visited over many surfing experiences, not just the most recent one.

To select a page from your bookmark list, pull down the **Bookmark/Favorites** menu and click on the desired entry. To save a favorite page location, use the Add feature available in both browsers. In Netscape Communicator, clicking on the **Add Bookmark** command makes a bookmark entry for the current page. **Add to Favorites** performs the same function in Microsoft Internet Explorer. Clicking this feature adds the location of the current page to your **Bookmark/Favorites** menu.

A cautionary note is in order here. Your bookmark or favorites list physically exists only on your personal computer, which means that if you connect to the Internet on a different computer, your list won't be available. If you routinely connect to the Internet from a computer lab, for example, get ready to carry the URLs for your favorite Web sites in your notebook or your head.

part

1

Searching and Search Engines

Returning to our cable television analogy, you may recall that we conveniently glossed over the question of how we selected a starting channel in the first place. With a million TV channels, or several million Web pages, we can't depend solely on luck guiding us to something interesting.

On the Web, we solve the problem with specialized computer programs called *search engines* that crawl through the Web, page by page, cataloging its contents. As different software designers developed search strategies, entrepreneurs established Web sites where any user could find pages containing particular words and phrases. Today, Web sites such as Yahoo!, AltaVista, Excite, WebCrawler, and HotBot offer you a "front door" to the Internet that begins with a search for content of interest.

The URLs for some popular search sites are:

Excite	`www.excite.com`
Yahoo!	`www.yahoo.com`
AltaVista	`www.altavista.digital.com`
WebCrawler	`www.webcrawler.com`
MetaCrawler	`www.metacrawler.com`
Infoseek	`www.infoseek.com`
HotBot	`www.hotbot.com`

Internet Gold Is Where You Find It

Let's perform a simple search using HotBot to find information about the history of the Internet.

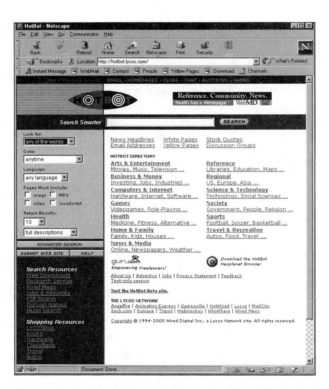

part **1**

We'll start by searching for the words "internet" or "history." By looking for "any of the words," the search will return pages on which either "internet" or "history" or both appear.

Our search returned more than 1,000,000 matches or *hits.* Pages are ranked according to the following factors: words in the title, keyword meta tags, word frequency in the document, and document length.

We can conduct the same search, but this time look for "all the words." The search will return hits when both "internet" and "history" appear on the same page, in any order, and not necessarily next to each other.

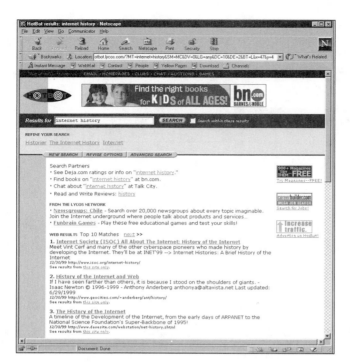

The search is narrowed down somewhat, but still has more than 1,000,000 hits.

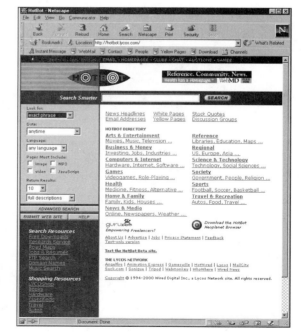

When we search for the exact phrase "internet history," which means those two words in exactly that order, with no intervening words, we're down to several thousand hits (still a substantial number).

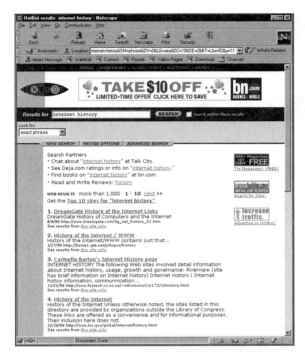

Now the first hits may be more specific. However, other hits in the list may have nothing to do with the history of the Internet. Hits happen. No search engine is 100 percent accurate 100 percent of the time. Spurious search results are the serendipity of the Internet. Look at them as an opportunity to explore something new.

Out of curiosity, let's try our history of the Internet search using a different search engine. When we search for the phrase "history of the internet" using WebCrawler, the quotation marks serve the same purpose as selecting "the exact phrase" option in Hotbot. The WebCrawler search only finds a few hundred hits. Some are the same as those found using HotBot, some are different. Different searching strategies and software algorithms make using more than one search engine a must for serious researchers.

The major search engines conveniently provide you with tips to help you get the most out of their searches. These include ways to use AND and OR to narrow down searches, and ways to use NOT to eliminate unwanted hits.

Each search engine also uses a slightly different approach to cataloging the Web, so at different sites your results might vary. Often, one search engine provides better results (more relevant hits) in your areas of interest; sometimes, the wise strategy is to provide the same input to several different engines. No one search engine does a perfect job all the time, so experience will dictate the one that's most valuable for you.

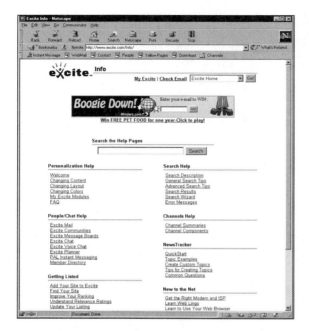

You'll find search tip pages like this at all the major search engine sites.

Quick Check

Let's review our searching strategies:

- ■ Visit one of the search engine sites;
- ■ Enter key words or phrases that best describe the search criteria;
- ■ Narrow the search if necessary by using options such as "all the words" or "the exact phrase." On some search engines, you may use the word "and" or the symbol "|" to indicate words that all must appear on a page;
- ■ Try using the same criteria with different search engines.

How Not to Come Down with a Virus

Downloading files from the Internet allows less responsible Net citizens to unleash onto your computer viruses, worms, and Trojan horses, all dangerous programs that fool you into thinking they're doing one thing while they're actually erasing your hard disk or performing some other undesirable task. Protection is your responsibility.

One way to reduce the risk of contracting a virus is to download software from reliable sites. Corporations such as Microsoft and Apple take care to make sure downloadable software is virus free. So do most institutions that provide software downloads as a public service (such as the Stanford University archives of Macintosh software). Be especially careful of programs you find on someone's home page. If you're not sure about safe download sources, ask around in a newsgroup (discussed shortly), talk to friends, or check with the information technology center on campus.

You can also buy and use a reliable virus program. Symantec and Dr. Solomon sell first-rate programs for the Mac and PC. You can update these programs right from the Internet so they'll detect the most current viruses. Most of the time, these programs can disinfect files/documents on your disk that contain viruses. Crude as it may sound, downloading programs from the Internet without using a virus check is like having unprotected sex with a stranger. While downloading software may not be life threatening, imagine the consequences if your entire hard disk, including all your course work and software, is totally obliterated. It won't leave you feeling very good.

part
1

The (E)mail Goes Through

Email was one of the first applications created for the Internet by its designers, who sought a method of communicating with each other directly from their keyboards. Your electronic Internet mailbox is to email what a post office box is to "snail mail" (the name Net citizens apply to ordinary, hand-delivered mail). This mailbox resides on the computer of your Internet Service Provider (ISP). That's the organization providing you with your Internet account. Most of the time your ISP will be your school; but, you may contract with one of the commercial providers, such as America Online, Mindspring, Microsoft Network, Earthlink, or AT&T. The Internet doesn't deliver a message to your door but instead leaves it in a conveniently accessible place (your mailbox) in the post office (the computer of your ISP), until you retrieve the mail using your combination (password).

If you currently have computer access to the Internet, your school or ISP assigned you a *user name* (also called a user id, account name, or account number). This user name may be your first name, your first initial and the first few characters of your last name, or some strange combination of numbers and letters only a computer could love. An email address is a combination of your user name and the unique address of the computer through which you access your email, like this:

```
username@computername.edu
```

The three letters after the dot, in this case "edu," identify the top level "domain." There are six common domain categories in use: edu (educational), com (commercial), org (organization), net (network), mil (military), and gov (government). The symbol "@"—called the "at" sign in typewriter days—serves two purposes: For computers, it provides a neat, clean separation between your user name and the computer name; for people, it makes Internet addresses more pronounceable. Your address is read: user name "at" computer name "dot" e-d-u. Suppose your Internet user name is "a4736g" and your ISP is Allyn & Bacon, the publisher of this book. Your email address might look like

```
a4736g@abacon.com
```

and you would tell people your email address is "ay-four-seven-three-six-gee at ay bacon dot com."

We Don't Just Handle Your Email, We're Also a Client

You use email with the aid of special programs called *mail clients*. As with search engines, mail clients have the same set of core features, but your access to these features varies with the type of program. On both the PC and the Mac, Netscape Communicator and Microsoft Internet Explorer give you access to mail clients while you're plugged into the Web. That way you can pick up and send mail while you're surfing the Web.

The basic email service functions are creating and sending mail, reading mail, replying to mail, and forwarding mail. First we'll examine the process of sending and reading mail, and then we'll discuss how to set up your programs so that your messages arrive safely.

Let's look at a typical mail client screen, in this case from Netscape Communicator 4.7. You reach this screen by choosing **Messenger** from under the **Communicator** menu. To send a message from scratch, choose the **New Msg** button to create a blank message form, which has fields for the recipient's address and the subject, and a window for the text of the message.

Fill in the recipient's address in the "To" field, just above the arrow. Use your own address. We'll send email to ourselves and use the same message to practice sending email and reading it as well; then we'll know if your messages come out as expected.

Click in the "Subject" field and enter a word or phrase that generally describes the topic of the message. Since we're doing this for the first time, let's type "Maiden Email Voyage."

Now click anywhere in the text window and enter your message. Let's say "Hi. Thanks for guiding me through sending my first email." You'll find that the mail client works here like a word processing program, which means you can insert and delete words and characters and highlight text.

Now click the **Send** button on the Navigation toolbar. You've just created and sent your first email message. In most systems, it takes a few seconds to a few minutes for a message to yourself to reach your mailbox, so you might want to take a short break before continuing. When you're ready to proceed, close the **Composition** window and click the **Get Msg** button.

part

1

New message form, with fields for recipient's address and the subject, and a window for the text of the message.

What Goes Around Comes Around

Now let's grab hold of the message you just sent to yourself. When retrieving mail, most mail clients display a window showing the messages in your mailbox telling you how many new messages have been added.

If you've never used your email before, chances are your message window is empty, or contains only one or two messages (usually official messages from the ISP) besides the one you sent to yourself. The message to yourself should be accompanied by an indicator of some sort—a colored mark, the letter N—indicating it's a new message. In Netscape Communicator, as in other mail clients, you also get to see the date of the message, who sent it, and the information you entered in the subject line. The Subject field lets you scan your messages and determine which ones you want to look at first.

The summary of received messages tells you everything you need to know about a message except what's in it. Click anywhere in the line to see the contents in the message window. Click on the message from yourself and you'll see the contents of the message displayed in a window. The information at the top—To, From, Subject, and so forth—is called the *header*. Depending on your system, you may also see some cryptic lines with terms such as X-Mailer, received by, and id number. Most of the time, there's nothing in this part of the header of interest, so just skip over it for now.

Moving Forward

The contents, or text, of your message can be cut and pasted just like any other text document. If you and a classmate are working on a project together, your partner can write part of a paper and email it to you, and you can copy the text from your email message and paste it into your word processing program.

What if there are three partners in this project? One partner sends you a draft of the paper for you to review. You like it and want to send it on to your other partner. The **Forward** feature lets you send the message intact, so you don't have to cut and paste it into a new message window. To forward a message, highlight it in the **Inbox** (top) and click the **Forward** icon. Enter the recipient's address in the "To" field of the message window. Note that the subject of the message is "Fwd:" followed by the subject of the original message. Use the text window to add your comments ahead of the original message.

A Chance to Reply

Email is not a one-way message system. Let's walk through a reply to a message from a correspondent named Elliot. Highlight the message in your **Inbox** again and this time click on the **Reply** icon. Depending on which program you're using, you'll see that each line in the message is preceded by either a vertical bar or a right angle bracket (>).

Note the "To" and "Subject" fields are filled in automatically with the address of the sender and the original subject preceded by "Re:". In Internet terminology, the message has been *quoted*. The vertical bar or > is used to indicate lines not written by you but by someone else (in this case, the message's original author). Why bother? Because this feature allows you to reply without retyping the parts of the message you're responding to. Because your typing isn't quoted, your answers stand out from the original message. Netscape Communicator 4.7 adds some blank lines above and below your comments, a good practice for you if your mail client doesn't do this automatically.

Welcome to the Internet, Miss Manners

While we're on the subject of email, here are some *netiquette* (net etiquette) tips.

- When you send email to someone, even someone who knows you well, all they have to look at are your words—there's no body language attached. That means there's no smile, no twinkle in the eye, no raised eyebrow; and especially, there's no tone of voice. What you write is open to interpretation and your recipient has nothing to guide him or her. You may understand the context of a remark, but will your reader? If you have any doubts about how your message will be interpreted, you might want to tack on an *emoticon* to your message. An emoticon is a face created out of keyboard characters. For example, there's the happy Smiley :-) (you have to look at it sideways . . . the parenthesis is its mouth), the frowning Smiley :-((Frownie?), the winking Smiley ;-), and so forth. Smileys are the body language of the Internet. Use them to put remarks in context. "Great," in response to a friend's suggestion means you like the idea. "Great :-(" changes the meaning to one of disappointment or sarcasm. (Want a complete list of emoticons? Try using "emoticon" as a key word for a Web search.)

▪ Keep email messages on target. One of the benefits of email is its speed. Reading through lengthy messages leaves the reader wondering when you'll get to the point.

▪ Email's speed carries with it a certain responsibility. Its ease of use and the way a messages seems to cry out for an answer both encourage quick responses, but quick doesn't necessarily mean thoughtful. Once you hit the **Send** icon, that message is gone. There's no recall button. Think before you write, lest you feel the wrath of the modern-day version of your parents' adage: Answer in haste, repent at leisure.

Keeping Things to Yourself

Here's another tip cum cautionary note, this one about Web security. Just as you take care to protect your wallet or purse while walking down a crowded street, it's only good practice to exercise caution with information you'd like to keep (relatively) private. Information you pass around the Internet is stored on, or passed along by, computers that are accessible to others. Although computer system administrators take great care to insure the security of this information, no scheme is completely infallible. Here are some security tips:

▪ Exercise care when sending sensitive information such as credit card numbers, passwords, even telephone numbers and addresses in plain email. Your email message may pass through four or five computers en route to its destination, and at any of these points, it can be intercepted and read by someone other than the recipient.

▪ Send personal information over the Web only if the page is secure. Web browsers automatically encrypt information on secure pages, and the information can only be unscrambled at the Web site that created the secure page. You can tell if a page is secure by checking the status bar at the bottom of your browser's window for an icon of a closed lock.

▪ Remember that any files you store on your ISP's computer are accessible to unscrupulous hackers.

▪ Protect your password. Many Web client programs, such as mail clients, have your password for you. That means anyone with physical access to your computer can read your email. With a few simple tools, someone can even steal your password. Never leave your password on a lab computer. (Make sure the **Remember Password** or **Save Password** box is unchecked in any application that asks for your password.)

The closed lock icon in the lower left-hand corner of your browser window indicates a "secure" Web page.

An Audience Far Wider Than You Imagine

Remember that the Web in particular and the Internet in general are communications mediums with a far-reaching audience, and placing information on the Internet is tantamount to publishing it. Certainly, the contents of any message or page you post become public information, but in a newsgroup (an electronic bulletin board), your email address also becomes public knowledge. On a Web page, posting a photo of your favorite music group can violate the photographer's copyright, just as if you published the image in a magazine. Use common sense about posting information you or someone else expects to remain private; and, remember, information on the Web can and will be read by people with different tastes and sensitivities. The Web tends to be self-censoring, so be prepared to handle feedback, both good and bad.

part

1

A Discussion of Lists

There's no reason you can't use email to create a discussion group. You pose a question, for example, by sending an email message to everyone in the group. Somebody answers and sends the answer to everyone else on the list, and so on.

At least, that's the theory.

In practice, this is what often happens. As people join and leave the group, you and the rest of your group are consumed with updating your lists, adding new names and deleting old ones. As new people join, their addresses may not make it onto the lists of all the members of the group, so different participants get different messages. The work of administering the lists becomes worse than any value anyone can get out of the group, and so it quickly dissolves.

Generally, you're better off letting the computer handle discussion group administration. A *list server* is a program for administering emailing lists. It automatically adds and deletes list members and handles the distribution of messages.

Thousands of mailing lists have already been formed by users with common interests. You may find mailing lists for celebrities, organizations, political interests, occupations, and hobbies. Your instructor may establish a mailing list for your course.

Groups come in several different flavors. Some are extremely active. You can receive as many as forty or more email messages a day. Other lists may send you a message a month. One-way lists, such as printed newsletters, do not distribute your reply to any other subscriber. Some lists distribute replies to everyone. These lists include mediated lists, in which an "editor" reviews each reply for suitability (relevance, tone, use of language) before distributing the message, and unmediated lists, in which each subscriber's response is automatically distributed to all the other subscribers with no restrictions except those dictated by decency

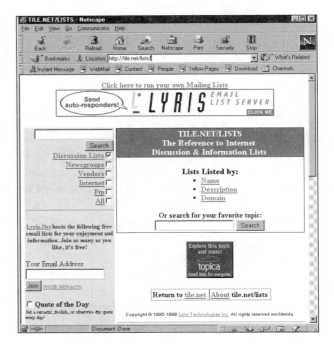

Tile.Net offfers shortcuts to working your way through the Internet's maze of discussion lists.

and common sense, though these qualities may not always be obvious from reading the messages.

Get on a List Online

You join in the discussion by subscribing to a list, which is as straightforward as sending email. You need to know only two items: the name of the list and the address of the list server program handling subscriptions. To join a list, send a **Subscribe** message to the list server address. The message is usually as simple as "subscribe," the name of the list, and your name (your real name, not your user name), all on one line. *And that's all.* This message will be read by a computer program that looks for these items only. At the very best, other comments in the message will be ignored. At the very worst, your entire message will be ignored, and so will you.

Within a few hours to a day after subscribing, the list server will automatically send you a confirmation email message, including instructions for sending messages, finding out information about the list and its members, and canceling your subscription. Save this message for future reference. That way, if you do decide to leave the list, you won't have to circulate a message to the members asking how to unsubscribe, and you won't have to wade through fifty replies all relaying the same information you received when you joined.

Soon after your confirmation message appears in your mailbox, and depending on the activity level of the list, you'll begin receiving email messages. New list subscribers customarily wait a while before joining the discussion. After all, you're electronically strolling into a room full of strangers; it's only fair to see what topics are being discussed before wading in with your own opinions. Otherwise, you're like the bore at the party who elbows his way into a conversation with "But enough about you, let's talk about me." You'll also want to avoid the faux pas of posting a long missive on a topic that subscribers spent the preceding three weeks thrashing out. Observe the list for a while, understand its tone and feel, what topics are of interest to others and what areas are taboo. Also, look for personalities. Who's the most vociferous? Who writes very little but responds thoughtfully? Who's the most flexible? The most rigid? Most of all, keep in mind that there are far more observers than participants. What you write may be read by 10 or 100 times more people than those whose names show up in the daily messages.

When you reply to a message, you reply to the list server address, not to the address of the sender (unless you intend for your communication to remain private). The list server program takes care of distributing

part
1

your message listwide. Use the address in the "Reply To" field of the message. Most mail clients automatically use this address when you select the **Reply** command. Some may ask if you want to use the reply address (say yes). Some lists will send a copy of your reply to you so you know your message is online. Others don't send the author a copy, relying on your faith in the infallibility of computers.

In the words of those famous late night television commercials, you can cancel your subscription at any time. Simply send a message to the address you used to subscribe (which you'll find on that confirmation message you saved for reference), with "unsubscribe," followed on the same line by the name of the list. For example, to leave a list named "WRITER-L," you would send:

```
unsubscribe WRITER-L
```

Even if you receive messages for a short while afterwards, have faith—they will disappear.

Waste Not, Want Not

List servers create an excellent forum for people with common interests to share their views; however, from the Internet standpoint, these lists are terribly wasteful. First of all, if there are one thousand subscribers to a list, every message must be copied one thousand times and distributed over the Internet. If there are forty replies a day, this one list creates forty thousand email messages. Ten such lists mean almost a half million messages, most of which are identical, flying around the Net.

Another wasteful aspect of list servers is the way in which messages are answered. The messages in your mailbox on any given day represent a combination of new topics and responses to previous messages. But where are these previous messages? If you saved them, they're in your email mailbox taking up disk space. If you haven't saved them, you have nothing to compare the response to. What if a particular message touches off a chain of responses, with subscribers referring not only to the source message but to responses as well? It sounds like the only safe strategy is to save every message from the list, a suggestion as absurd as it is impractical.

What we really need is something closer to a bulletin board than a mailing list. On a bulletin board, messages are posted once. Similar notices wind up clustered together. Everyone comes to the same place to read or post messages.

And Now the News(group)

The Internet equivalent of the bulletin board is the Usenet or newsgroup area. Usenet messages are copied only once for each ISP supporting the newsgroup. If there are one thousand students on your campus reading the same newsgroup message, there need only be one copy of the message stored on your school's computer.

Categorizing a World of Information

Newsgroups are categorized by topics, with topics broken down into subtopics and sub-subtopics. For example, you'll find newsgroups devoted to computers, hobbies, science, social issues, and "alternatives." Newsgroups in this last category cover a wide range of topics that may not appeal to the mainstream. Also in this category are beginning newsgroups.

Usenet names are amalgams of their topics and subtopics, separated by dots. If you were interested in a newsgroup dealing with, say, music, you might start with rec.music and move down to rec.music.radiohead, or rec.music.techno, and so forth. The naming scheme allows you to zero in on a topic of interest.

part

1

Getting into the News(group) Business

Most of the work of reading, responding to, and posting messages is handled by a news reader client program, accessible through both Netscape Communicator and Microsoft Internet Explorer. You can not only surf the Web and handle your mail via your browser, but you can also drop into your favorite newsgroups virtually all in one operation.

Let's drop into a newsgroup. To reach groups via Netscape Communicator 4.7, go to the Communicator menu bar and select **Newsgroups.** Then, from the File menu, select **Subscribe.** A dialogue box will open that displays a list of available groups.

To subscribe to a newsgroup—that is, to tell your news reader you want to be kept up-to-date on the messages posted to a particular group—highlight the group of interest and click on **Subscribe.** Alternately, you can click in the Subscribe column to the right of the group name. The check mark in the Subscribe column means you're "in."Now, click **OK.**

The message center in Netscape Communicator displays a list of newsgroups on your subscription list. Double click on the one of current interest and your reader presents you with a list of messages posted on the group's bulletin board. Double click on a message to open its contents in a window.

Often, messages contain "Re:" in their subject lines, indicating a response to a previous message (the letters stand for "Regarding"). Many news readers maintain a *thread* for you. Threads are chains of messages and all responses to that message. These readers give you the option to read messages chronologically or to read a message followed by its responses.

part

1

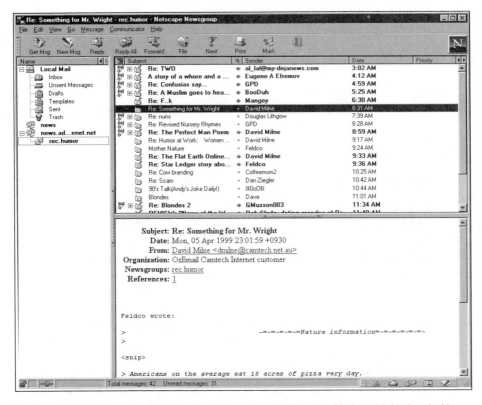

The top part of this figure shows a listing of posted messages. While not visible from this black and white reproduction, a red indicator in the Subject column marks unread messages. Double-clicking on a message opens its contents into a window shown in the bottom part of this figure. You can reply to this message via the Reply icon, or get the next message using the Next icon.

When you subscribe to a newsgroup, your news reader will also keep track of the messages you've read so that it can present you with the newest (unread) ones. While older messages are still available to you, this feature guarantees that you stay up-to-date without any record keeping on your part. Subscribing to a newsgroup is free, and the subscription information resides on your computer.

Newsgroups have no way of knowing who their subscribers are, and the same caveat that applies to bookmarks applies to newsgroups. Information about your subscriptions resides physically on the personal computer you're using. If you switch computers, as in a lab, your subscription information and history of read messages are beyond your reach.

Welcome to the Internet, Miss Manners—Again

As with list servers, hang out for a while, or *lurk,* to familiarize yourself with the style, tone, and content of newsgroup messages. As you probably surmised from the names of the groups, their topics of discussion are quite narrow. One of the no-nos of newsgroups is posting messages on subjects outside the focus of the group. Posting off-topic messages, especially lengthy ones, is an excellent way to attract a flaming.

A *flame* is a brutally debasing message from one user to another. Flames are designed to hurt and offend, and often the target of the flame feels compelled to respond in kind to protect his or her self-esteem. This leads to a *flame war,* as other users take sides and wade in with flames of their own. If you find yourself the target of a flame, your best strategy is to ignore it. As with a campfire, if no one tends to the flames, they soon die out.

As mentioned earlier, posting messages to newsgroups is a modern form of publishing, and a publisher assumes certain responsibilities. You have a duty to keep your messages short and to the point. Many newsgroup visitors connect to the Internet via modems. Downloading a day's worth of long postings, especially uninteresting ones, is annoying and frustrating. Similarly, don't post the same message to multiple, related newsgroups. This is called *cross posting,* and it's a peeve of Net citizens who check into these groups. If you've ever flipped the television from channel to channel during a commercial break only to encounter the same commercial (an advertising practice called *roadblocking*), you can imagine how annoying it is to drop in on several newsgroups only to find the same messages posted to each one.

part

1

With the huge potential audience newsgroups offer, you might think you've found an excellent medium for advertising goods or services. After all, posting a few messages appears analogous to running classified ads in newspapers, only here the cost is free. There's a name for these kinds of messages—*spam*. Spam is the junk mail of the Internet, and the practice of spamming is a surefire way to attract flames. The best advice for handling spam? Don't answer it. Not only does an answer encourage the spammer, but he or she will also undoubtedly put your email address on a list and sell it to other spammers, who will flood your online mailbox with their junk.

Above all, be considerate of others. Treat them the way you'd like to be treated. Do you enjoy having your grammar or word choices corrected in front of the whole world? Do you feel comfortable when someone calls you stupid in public? Do you appreciate having your religion, ethnicity, heritage, or gender belittled in front of an audience? Respect the rights and feelings of others, if not out of simple decency then out of the sanctions your ISP may impose. Although you have every right to express an unpopular opinion or to take issue with the postings of others, most ISPs have regulations about the kinds of messages one can send via their facilities. Obscenities, threats, and spam may, at a minimum, result in your losing your Internet access privileges.

part

1

Give Your Web Browser Some Personality—Yours

Before accessing email and newsgroup functions, you need to set up or personalize your browser. If you always work on the same personal computer, this is a one-time operation that takes only a few minutes. In it, you tell your browser where to find essential computer servers, along with personal information the Internet needs to move messages for you.

- *Step 1:* Open the **Preferences** menu in Netscape or the **Internet Options** in Internet Explorer. In Netscape Communicator the Preferences menu is located under the **Edit** menu; in Microsoft Internet Explorer the Internet Options can be found under the **View** menu.

- *Step 2:* Tell the browser who you are and where to find your mail servers. Your Reply To address is typically the same as your email address, though if you have an email alias you can use it here. Your ISP will provide the server names and addresses. SMTP handles your outgoing messages, while the POP3 server routes incoming mail. Often, but not always, these server names are the same.

■ *Step 3:*   Tell the browser where to find your news server. Your ISP will furnish the name of the server. Note that in Microsoft Internet Explorer, you specify a helper application to read the news. Now that most computers come with browsers already loaded onto the hard disk, you'll find that these helper applications are already set up for you.

■ *Step 4:*   Set your home page. For convenience, you may want your browser to start by fetching a particular page, such as your favorite search site. Or you might want to begin at your school library's home page. Enter the URL for this starting page in the home page address field. Both Netscape and Microsoft offer the option of no home page when you start up. In that case, you get a blank browser window.

Operating systems such as Mac OS 8 or 9 and Microsoft Windows 95, 98, and 2000 offer automated help in setting up your browsers for Web, mail, and newsgroup operation. You need to know the names of the servers mentioned above, along with your user name and other details, such as the address of the domain name server (DNS) of your ISP. You should receive all this information when you open your Internet account. If not, ask for it.

part
1

Why Sociology and the Internet?

By now, like a growing number of people, you've likely visited cyberspace. If you haven't, your experience will happen sooner or later. No doubt the fact that you're reading this puts your Internet journey in the "sooner" category. In this section we'd like to look at three things. First, let's look at the added value gained by the use of the Internet when you're learning sociology. Then, we'll examine the Internet–sociology relationship in the development of the sociological perspective and the application of sociology to real life issues. Finally, we want you to consider some reasons why you might not want to use the Net. In this part we'll try to provide some ideas for approaching the material that is so easy to find. Let's take these in turn.

Added Value

■ Sociology's strength and weakness: its breadth.

You've learned that sociology is a very broad subject. On one extreme, you're viewing the interaction between two people on a sidewalk. On another extreme, you're looking at the interaction among cultures! It's a fairly comprehensive approach. This is impressive and valuable. Sociologists want us to look at the big picture. We want you to understand that human action occurs in context. While this is a comprehensive and, I might add, attractive view, it has its weaknesses. While it is possible and challenging to think about this vast spectrum of human social life, it is often difficult to investigate the diverse topics that you would normally find in a sociology course. Professional sociologists have experienced this problem, too. That is why sociologists often focus on a specific area within the field (race and ethnicity, stratification, applied sociology, demography or criminology, for example). While the Internet does not solve the problem of this complexity, it does give us a handy place to start. Here's what we mean.

part

■ The Internet allows sociologists and students of sociology to expand their horizons.

The Net makes it possible to examine the breadth of sociology. Instead of just talking about human interaction at all levels, we can visit and sometimes even experience this vast range of social adventure. The Internet has provided a means for us to view, first hand, the breadth of sociology. We can imagine it and we can experience it. Now, early in the process of learning sociology and the sociological perspective, we can actively engage the world we are trying to understand. This leads us to another point.

■ Sociological concepts are expressed in general terms.

Sociological concepts and ideas are general and generalizing in their nature. If you (like us) have muttered to yourself, "That's not true for everybody!" then you understand this. When exposed to some sociological finding, you're probably not alone. Of course, "true for everybody" is not what sociologists are trying to point out. It takes a rather long period of time for the sociological perspective to mature. The broad nature of sociology and the broadening nature of its vocabulary often leave students with a feeling that they "can't grab it" or rather that they're "putting their hands through it." We're making the case that sociology needs to be made as concrete as it can be to enhance understanding. Accessing examples directly via the Internet can assist us in this effort. One of the things we suddenly learn is that we're working with dynamic subject matter.

- The dynamic nature of society becomes apparent.

The Web helps provide evidence for and examples of some of the sociological principles that you're learning. In many ways it can empower you to think critically as you interpret evidence. You'll find yourself effectively able to gather information that challenges assertions made by other students and your instructors! By having instantaneous access to large amounts of information, you can critically think about, and then investigate, an idea. The Net is another valuable tool for active learning. You can engage the world directly, apply the sociological principles you've learned, and then make your own decisions about sociology's value. Finally, the dynamic nature of the Net is a sociologic example. You only need to go to a Web site and find: "File Not Found," to realize that you're working with a dynamic social phenomenon. The Internet changes, moment to moment. It in itself is an example of the nature of the focus of sociological interest and imagination. We've tried to provide a current set of links to Web sites in this booklet, but as anyone who has been on the Web or has written Internet courses (you're welcome to visit the author's introductory course on http://www.aacc.cc.md.us/sociology/ soc111start.htm) will tell you, as soon as you put anything in writing about the Net, it changes!

part

1

Development of the Sociological Perspective and the Application of Sociology

- The Internet lets you "do sociology" early in your entrance into the field.

We know that most of you may never take another sociology course. Plain and simple, most people don't become sociology majors (even if we would like you to). That's why we're particularly enthusiastic about the Net's capacity to enhance the application of sociology to real world problems. We've tried to provide some applied exercises that demonstrate the direct value of the perspective in understanding and addressing a variety of social conditions. This can only enhance your personal and sociological growth. Like any pursuit, sociology needs to be practiced from the start to be understood. We need to know it, feel it, and do it, to best understand it. Also, like any pursuit, this maturation occurs over a lifetime, yet the sooner you engage *what* you've learned, the sooner you add experience to your life repertoire. We hope that when you finish this course you'll walk away with added tools and experiences to enhance your life and your career.

■ You realize that sociology has an applied side.

"It's neat stuff, but what can I do with it?" The authors have heard this too many times when first-time sociology students come head-to-head with our perspectives and principles. It's a good question and a challenging one. In our view, sociologists need to supply some kind of an answer. We're answering with an approach that is fostered by the active nature of the Internet. Sociology can be "done." But sociology doesn't exist in a vacuum! Its tools must be integrated with other life and professional skills. Since sociology investigates human social life, we can also prosper from borrowing and learning from the valid tools and perspectives of the world we study. When we focus on applying sociology to a real world problem, we begin to realize that sociology adds value to the understanding of the problem. But a sociological view is not the only view, and because "dealing with the problem" is central, we become respectful of the valid perspectives of other professionals—psychologists, economists, business persons, policy analysts, clergy, human resources professionals, and community leaders, to name a few. The Net provides a means for us to mature sociologically through knowledge and action.

Reasons Why You Might Not Want to Use the Net

After reading this, you no doubt believe that we think the Internet is extraordinary. As a social phenomenon, as an agent of empowerment and as a tool for understanding sociology, the Net is very important. But there are some very important reasons why you might not want to use the Net. Let's look at some of them.

■ The Net does not replace thinking—it's easy to drown in information.

Finding links to information does not replace thoughtfully thinking about that information. The doubling time on Internet information shortens almost daily. It becomes virtually (pun?) impossible to keep up with its limits. At the same time, it becomes easy to be swamped with information. You can simply get too much information. Having and engaging Web access does not guarantee that you'll make sense out of what you have found. In fact, it has become even more important to clearly think about and clarify the problem that you are investigating. The process may be a little different now. The Net can be used as a way to inductively engage a problem: look at what's out there, categorize it, and begin to frame a problem. Or more traditionally, and still a good bet, state and clarify the problem that you plan to investigate as clearly as you can first, and then go to the Internet to search. Regardless, the burden of analysis and interpretation falls on the shoulders of thinking, reasoning persons. Finding links to information does not replace careful thinking about that information.

■ There's lots of garbage out there and you need to sort it out.

In closing, we'd like to remind you that there's lots of garbage on the Net. It comes in a variety of forms. Sometimes we'll remind you to check the following "garbage detectors" in the exercises that follow. If we don't, we hope you will be guided by the following when you open an Internet link:

part

1

a. **Who runs this site?**   Consider the source of the information. Your sociological training has no doubt provided you with a critical eye. Individuals and organizations have some point of view even if it is objectivity. Be sure you consider the originator of the site. How do this organization's or individual's values creep into the information on the site? Why are they putting this on the Internet?

b. **Is this what you want?**   Consider the information itself. Does it really address the problem that you have identified? Is it timely and understandable?

c. **Are there other sources that would be better?**   Here are two quick examples of what we mean. (1) Consider a book . . . no, we mean it! Remember that in a twenty-first century world a book still has a great deal going for it. It's portable, relatively inexpensive, adds beauty to your bookshelf, provides a tactual experience (you can actually hold it) and it can be read just about anywhere and anytime. You can "dog-ear" it, write in it, and come directly back to the parts that make sense. (2) Consider talking to people. This is a bold plan! While electronic communication is important, face-to-face transfer of information is qualitatively unique. Remember that sociology is about human interaction—all forms.

A Beginning

This booklet is a beginning. We couldn't hope to cover every topic in sociology, every theoretical point of view and every corner of the discipline. Nor could we cover the vast expanses of human social life, including the Internet. So this booklet provides a beginning. Add sites, explore links and use your sociological imagination!

Critical Evaluation

Where Seeing Is Not Always Believing

Typical research resources, such as journal articles, books, and other scholarly works, are reviewed by a panel of experts before being published. At the very least, any reputable publisher takes care to assure that the author is who he or she claims to be and that the work being published represents a reasoned and informed point of view. When anyone can post anything in a Web site or to a newsgroup, the burden of assessing the relevance and accuracy of what you read falls to you. Rumors quickly grow into facts on the Internet simply because stories can spread so rapidly that the "news" seems to be everywhere. Because the Internet leaves few tracks, in no time it's impossible to tell whether you are reading independent stories or the merely same story that's been around the world two or three times. Gathering information on the Internet may be quick, but verifying the quality of information requires a serious commitment.

Approach researching via the Internet with confidence, however, and not with trepidation. You'll find it an excellent workout for your critical evaluation skills; no matter what career you pursue, employers value an employee who can think critically and independently. Critical thinking is also the basis of problem solving, another ability highly valued by the business community. So, as you research your academic projects, be assured that you're simultaneously developing lifelong expertise.

It's Okay to Be Critical of Others

The first tip for successful researching on the Internet is to always consider your source. A Web site's URL often alerts you to the sponsor of the site. CNN or MSNBC are established news organizations, and you can give the information you find at their sites the same weight you would give to their cablecasts. Likewise, major newspapers operate Web sites with articles reprinted from their daily editions or expanded stories written expressly for the Internet. On the other hand, if you're unfamiliar with the source, treat the information the way you would any new data. Look for specifics—"66 percent of all voters" as opposed to "most voters"—and for information that can be verified—a cited report in another medium or information accessible through a Web site hosted by a credible sponsor—as opposed to generalities or unverifiable claims. Look for independent paths to the same information. This can involve careful use of search engines or visits to newsgroups with both similar and opposing viewpoints. Make sure that the "independent" information you find is truly independent. In newsgroups don't discount the possibility of multiple postings, or that a posting in one group is nothing more than a quotation from a posting in another. Ways to verify independent paths include following sources (if any) back to their origins, contacting the person posting a message and asking for clarification, or checking other media for verification.

part

1

In many cases, you can use your intuition and common sense to raise your comfort level about the soundness of the information. With both list servers and newsgroups, it's possible to lurk for a while to develop a feeling for the authors of various postings. Who seems the most authoritarian, and who seems to be "speaking" from emotion or bias? Who seems to know what he or she is talking about on a regular basis? Do these people cite their sources of information (a job or affiliation perhaps)? Do they have a history of thoughtful, insightful postings, or do their postings typically contain generalities, unjustifiable claims, or flames? On Web sites, where the information feels more anonymous, there are also clues you can use to test for authenticity. Verify who's hosting the Web site. If the host or domain name is unfamiliar to you, perhaps a search engine can help you locate more information. Measure the tone and style of the writing at the site. Does it seem consistent with the education level and knowledge base necessary to write intelligently about the subject?

When offering an unorthodox point of view, good authors supply facts, figures, and quotes to buttress their positions, expecting readers to be skeptical of their claims. Knowledgeable authors on the Internet follow these same commonsense guidelines. Be suspicious of authors who expect you to agree with their points of view simply because they've published them on the Internet. In one-on-one encounters, you frequently judge the authority and knowledge of the speaker using criteria you'd be hard pressed to explain. Use your sense of intuition on the Internet, too.

As a researcher (and as a human being), the job of critical thinking requires a combination of healthy skepticism and rabid curiosity. Newsgroups and Web sites tend to focus narrowly on single issues (newsgroups more so than Web sites). Don't expect to find a torrent of opposing views on newsgroup postings; their very nature and reason for existence dampens free-ranging discussions. A newsgroup on *The X-Files* might argue about whether extraterrestrials exist but not whether the program is the premier television show on the air today. Such a discussion would run counter to the purposes of the newsgroup and would be a violation of netiquette. Anyone posting such a message would be flamed, embarrassed, ignored, or otherwise driven away. Your research responsibilities include searching for opposing views by visiting a variety of newsgroups and Web sites. A help here is to fall back on the familiar questions of journalism: who, what, when, where, and why.

part

1

■ **Who** else might speak knowledgeably on this subject? Enter that person's name into a search engine. You might be surprised to find whose work is represented on the Web. (For fun, one of the authors entered the name of a rock-and-roll New York radio disk jockey into MetaCrawler and was amazed to find several pages devoted to the DJ, including sound clips of broadcasts dating back to the sixties, along with a history of his theme song.)

■ **What** event might shed more information on your topic? Is there a group or organization that represents your topic? Do they hold an annual conference? Are synopses of presentations posted on the sponsoring organization's Web site?

■ **When** do events happen? Annual meetings or seasonal occurrences can help you isolate newsgroup postings of interest.

■ **Where** might you find this information? If you're searching for information on wines, for example, check to see if major wine-producing regions, such as the Napa Valley in California or the Rhine Valley in Germany, sponsor Web sites. These may point you to organizations or information that don't show up in other searches. Remember, Web search engines are fallible; they don't find every site you need.

- **Why** is the information you're searching for important? The answer to this question can lead you to related fields. New drugs, for example, are important not only to victims of diseases but to drug companies and the FDA as well.

Approach assertions you read from a skeptic's point of view. See if they stand up to critical evaluation or if you're merely emotionally attached to them. Imagine "What if . . . ?" or "What about . . . ?" scenarios that may disprove or at least call into question what you're reading. Try following each assertion you pull from the Internet with the phrase, "On the other hand. . . ." Because you can't leave the sentence hanging, you'll be forced to finish it, and this will help get you into the habit of critically examining information.

These are, of course, the same techniques critical thinkers have employed for centuries, only now you are equipped with more powerful search tools than past researchers may have ever imagined. In the time it took your antecedents to formulate their questions, you can search dozens of potential information sources. You belong to the first generation of college students to enjoy both quantity and quality in its research, along with a wider perspective on issues and the ability to form personal opinions after reasoning from a much wider knowledge base. Certainly, the potential exists for the Internet to grind out a generation of intellectual robots, "thinkers" who don't think but who regurgitate information from many sources. Technology always has its good and bad aspects. However, we also have the potential to become some of the most well-informed thinkers in the history of the world, thinkers who are not only articulate but confident that their opinions have been distilled from a range of views, processed by their own personalities, beliefs, and biases. This is one of the aspects of the Internet that makes this era such an exciting combination of humanism and technology.

part

1

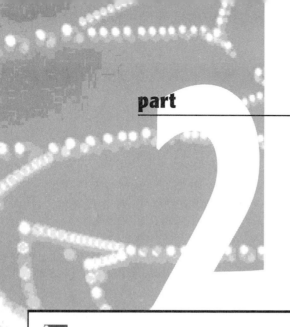

Internet Activities for Introduction to Sociology

Sociological Perspective 1

Overview

How do sociologists see the world? "What difference does it make to me?" you might ask. Let's examine the sociological perspective to see how it differs from other views of human social life.

Activity

Do you read a newspaper everyday? Your answer to this question is certainly a matter of personal choice. Whether you answer yes or no, a sociologist would no doubt be curious about your response. But, more likely a sociologist might ask a variety of questions. Are you like other Americans? What is happening to newspaper readership in our society? What forces produce this outcome?

Check the General Social Survey on **http://www.icpsr.umich.edu/gss/trend/news.htm**

These data are presented in a table generated by a frequently used statistical package (SPSS). Look at the row (remember rows go across, columns go up and down) labeled EVERYDAY. For every year that data are presented, record the year and the percent of people who say they read a newspaper every day. Now answer the following:

1. For the most recent year, are most Americans like you in terms of daily readership?

2. Over the years for which data were collected, what is happening to the percentage of people who read a newspaper everyday? Now, use your sociological imagination—What are some of the social factors that have caused this?

If you're responding in general categories of factors (increased television viewing, more computers, etc.), you're probably thinking more sociologically.

Sociological Perspective 2

Overview

The sociological perspective is handy because it can be applied to so many different and interesting areas. Think about it for a minute. What areas could use a little sociology? Let's take a look at a list.

part
2

Activity

1. List some areas that interest you that you believe could be viewed sociologically.

2. Now, go to **http://www.pscw.uva.nl/sociosite/TOPICS/index.html**

3. Is there anything on your list that matches here? If so, click on it and review the findings.

4. If you can't make a connection, choose 3–5 of the ones at the site and follow the links. There's no telling where these links might lead!

5. What are the strengths and weaknesses of sociology's breadth?

Sociological Perspective 3

Overview

How do sociologists know anything? Sociologists are scientists who study human interaction at many levels. The methods and techniques employed usually fall into two categories: quantitative and qualitative. Let's compare these two research approaches

Activity

Let's start by looking at a common "quantitative" method used by sociologists: the survey. Go to **http://hammock.ifas.ufl.edu/txt/fairs/13467**

1. Read the discussion on selecting a data collection technique.

2. Now, move to the middle of the page and click on "comparison of three techniques."

3. What are the three survey techniques described here? How are they similar and different? Under what circumstances is it best to use each?

   Now, let's turn to a common qualitative technique: focus groups. Go to **http://palette.ecn.purdue.edu/~ie486/Class/Lecture/lect13/index.htm**

4. What is a focus group?

   Then, go to **http://mime1.marc.gatech.edu/mm_tools/evaluation. html** Scroll down to "Focus Group." Read the overview and go to the protocol. Using information from both links, answer the following:

5. How do focus groups compare with surveys? How are they similar and how are they different?

6. How could the two techniques complement each other?

Sociological Perspective 4

Overview

Sociology and sociologists maintain a vast network of resources, organizations, and individuals that support the field. Let's explore some of the organizations that support sociology.

Activity

To get an initial view of the breadth of sociological organizations and resources, go to **http://www.princeton.edu/~sociolog/links.html**

1. Spend some time just investigating the information on this site.

2. Now, summarize the basic categories of information that you've found here.

3. Finally, make some comparisons:

   a. Compare two or more professional associations.

   b. Compare two or more regional associations, and

   c. Compare two or more organizations in different international locations.

4. Summarize your thoughts on the nature of the variety of these organizations.

Sociological Perspective 5

Overview

By now you are probably aware of sociology's breadth. The field easily extends from the interaction among "selves" to the interaction among societies. Let's get an understanding of the variety of topics that a professional sociologist might investigate.

Activity

One place to start is to identify the largest single professional organization for sociologists, the American Sociological Association. Go to **http://www.asanet.org/**

1. Once you have arrived, click on the list of sections in the ASA. Go to **http://www.asanet.org/Sections/general.htm**

2. What are sections? What value do they have?

3. How many sections did you find? Pick 3–5 sections that might appear to be interesting to you. Why would these be of interest?

4. Use your sociological imagination—What do you think sociologists in each section investigate? Some of the sections are linked to the web site. Explore the ones that interest you.

Other Sites on Sociological Perspective	
URL Link	**Summary: Who runs the site? Description?**

Applied Sociology 1

Overview

Practicing sociologists (and many other professionals as well) are called on to conduct program evaluations. After investing time, money and resources in a project, it would not be surprising or unreasonable to ask if the project "did what it was supposed to do." Evaluation skills are useful tools.

Activity

Go to the American Evaluation Association site at: **http://www.eval.org/** Evaluation design requires guidelines for implementation. Click on AEA Guiding Principles for Evaluators **http://www.eval.org/aeaprin6.html**

1. What are the major categories of guidelines that are recommended for project or program evaluation?

2. What are some of the sociological perspectives and methods that might be used in an evaluation?

3. What would be some of the obstacles for performing a good evaluation?

Applied Sociology 2

Overview

Whether you're presenting your sociological information to an academic audience or a business client, making a good presentation is essential. Having some basic presentation skills can be extremely valuable.

Activity

First, let's find something to present. Go to **http://nces.ed.gov/ pubsearch/pubsinfo.asp?pubid=2000022**

1. Review the material on this site. What are the key variables and information presented here?

Now, suppose you need to make a presentation of the findings on this site to a group of businessmen and businesswomen who have assembled because of their concern for providing realistic work opportunities for dropouts. How would you do it? Go to **http://angelfire.com/hi/rwm/ presentation.html**

2. Review this site for pointers that would help you make your presentation.

3. Provide a brief outline of your presentation employing some of the suggestions on this site.

Applied Sociology 3

Overview

Practicing sociology means identifying, investigating and solving problems. There are many processes for problem analysis that can be valuable tools for you regardless of the career that you seek. Let's look at one of these.

Activity

Investigate the process for analyzing problems on **http://www. changedynamics.com/samples/probsolv.htm**

1. Review the process. What are its basic steps?

2. Compare this to the scientific method. How is it similar? How is it different?

3. Now, select a problem (whether from your workplace, college, family or your imagination). Use this process to analyze it.

4. What are the strengths and weaknesses of this process?

Other Sites on Applied Sociology	
URL Link	**Summary: Who runs the site? Description?**

part

2

How Sociologists Do Research 1

Overview

While sociologists and other social scientists often debate over the best tools to do research, none would doubt the wide variety of tools that are available. Let's turn to this large toolbox for a moment.

Activity

Go to **http://www.siu.edu/~hawkes/methods.html** Review the large spectrum of tools that are available to sociologists.

1. Sociologists need to learn a vast repertoire of tools and skills to do their work. What are some of the techniques and skills that look interesting to you?

2. Now, do a quick content analysis of the items that appear on this page. What categories of tools do sociologists need to learn?

How Sociologists Do Research 2

Overview

part
2Sociologists are social scientists. If we emphasize the science part of social sciences, we realize that sociologists have a great deal in common with all scientists: biologists, psychologists, physicists, chemists, anthropologists, etc. The common thread is the use of the scientific method. Let's review this perspective.

Activity

Here are some websites that address the scientific method. What do they have in common?

Biology: **http://www.an.psu.edu/jxm57/sci_inv1.html**

Field research: **http://www.sru.edu/depts/artsci/ges/fstudies/ scmeth.htm**

Forms of the Scientific Method: **http://www.twingroves.district96. k12.il.us/ScienceInternet/ ScientificMethod.html**

How Sociologists Do Research 3

Overview

Sociologists are known for doing survey research. While surveys aren't the only research method that we use, they are a valuable and common tool.

Activity

Survey research and its related skill, question writing, are difficult tasks. Part of the craft of becoming a sociologist is the ability to write good survey instruments. Before one can even write a good question, a researcher will need to reflect on a variety of factors influencing a survey. Go to **http://hammock.ifas.ufl.edu/txt/fairs/13467** Now answer the following questions:

1. What are reliability and validity? How do reliability and validity influence survey construction?

2. What is bias? How does bias impact on survey construction?

3. Now click on "Comparison of three techniques." Compare and contrast the three types of surveys identified here. State a research problem that could best be dealt with for each type of technique.

How Sociologists Do Research 4

Overview

Social scientists use a variety of tools to analyze data. Graphic and statistical tools are essential. This is a situation in which a few good tools can be extremely powerful.

Activity

In almost every data gathering experience you'll need to run some descriptive statistics. Go to **http://www.medschool.lsumc.edu/biom/ppt/ bascstat/tsld035.htm** and review the measures of central tendency. Since sociologists are interested in one number that stands for a group, these will be helpful.

Sometimes it's easier if we have a picture of information. Go to **http://www.twingroves.district96.k12.il.us/ScienceInternet/ ChartsGraphs.html** Scroll down to the middle of the page and review bar graphs, line graphs and circles (pie) graphs.

How Sociologists Do Research 5

Overview

Let's use this basic research tool, the survey, to deal with an application of the sociological perspective to a real life situation.

Activity

Go to **http://hammock.ifas.ufl.edu/txt/fairs/13471** and complete the following: You are an applied sociologist employed by a human resources department for a local hospital. The vice president of human resources has asked you to determine the level of worker satisfaction at all occupational levels in the hospital. You have two weeks to report your findings to the vice president. You decide to use a survey research technique. Apply the information in this link and decide which survey technique you would use and why you would use it.

part
2

Other Sites on How Sociologists Do Research	
URL Link	**Summary: Who runs the site? Description?**

Culture 1

Overview

Culture is a way of life and while each individual acts that way of life a little differently, we can improve our interaction with persons across cultures if we understand and respect the "ways" of life in which we find ourselves. This is one of the great strengths of sociology. Let's see how understanding culture can be of value to you.

Activity

You've decided to do some cross cultural consulting and determine that you would be better off if you met your clients in person rather than by Internet or telephone. Before you go on your trip, go to **http://www.worldculture.com/**

part

2

1. Select three countries outside the United States that you plan to visit on your business trip.

2. For each country, review each of the following:

   a. Cuisine

   b. Currency

   c. Language

   d. Gestures

   e. Religion

   f. Select one or more items of your choice.

3. Compare and contrast the countries you have selected on the items listed above.

4. How would these differences influence your interaction with your client?

Culture 2

Overview

Review the concept of culture. While sociologists and anthropologists often use this idea at a global level, it has other uses as well. Review the concepts that relate to culture: norms, values, beliefs, ethnocentrism, and cultural relativity. Then, work on the activity that follows.

Activity

Review three of the descriptions of the companies on this website: **http://www.workfamily.com/culture.htm** Think of each company as a corporate culture. That is, each company has its own culture within. While we can't be completely sure from the description provided, assess each of the cultures for the companies that you have selected. Indicate:

part

2

1. The difference in the way of life in each culture.

2. The core values or central things that appear to be valued in each.

3. What would it be like to work for these companies?

4. How would the culture influence the way that work is done in each?

Culture 3

Overview

Comparing cultures is difficult. As you are learning, ways of life vary greatly. Traveling internationally will challenge your views of other cultures and your own. Let's make some comparisons.

Activity

Nations are not quite the same as cultures, but you can get a sense of cultural difference by comparing national similarities and differences. Go to **http://www.odci.gov/cia/publications/nsolo/wfb-all.htm**
Do the following:

1. What is the source of this web site? Any thoughts?

2. Now select two different continents in turn. Now select one country on each continent.

3. What categories of information are provided for each country?

4. Now compare and contrast the two countries across the categories of information provided?

5. How are they similar and different?

6. Now use your sociological imagination—What would it be like to live in each?

Other Sites on Culture	
URL Link	**Summary: Who runs the site? Description?**

Socialization 1

Overview

Many factors influence the socialization of youth in a society. What are these factors? What impact do they have? Let's look at some indicators of youth in the United States.

part

2

Activity

Let's view a younger segment of the population. Go to **http://nces.ed.gov/pubs/yi/index.html**

1. Who runs this site? This site views 69 youth indicators. What are *indicators*? What are the categories of the indicators that you find here?

2. Now select at least one indicator from each category, click on it and review the data.

3. For each indicator that you have chosen, do the following:

   a. Write a brief 2–3 sentence paragraph that summarizes the condition presented by this indicator.

   b. Now use your sociological imagination: What impact will this have on the lives of the youth presented?

4. What are the strengths and weaknesses of assessing the condition of youth by using this indicator's strategy?

part

2

Socialization 2

Overview

Socialization is a process in which norms, values, and beliefs are passed to another person. In this process, this individual person becomes a social self. This process is life-long and we are often resocialized. Let's compare some processes and programs that intend to resocialize people.

Activity

Browse and compare the resocialization that is presented or discussed in each of the following three sites.

1. Compare and contrast the similarities and differences in the target (who?) of the resocialization, purpose, method, and anticipated outcomes for each.

   http://www.tyc.state.tx.us/index.html (Click on "Basic Correctional Treatment–Resocialization")

http://www.parent-education.com/about.html

http://www.unicor.gov/placement/

How effective do you believe that each will be in resocializing? What social forces influence the success of this resocialization?

Other Sites on Socialization	
URL Link	**Summary: Who runs the site? Description?**

part

2

Social Structure 1

Overview

Social structure is a term sociologists use often. The term implies action driven by norms; persistent, patterned, organized action. These established and systematized patterns produce predictable outcomes. At a macro level, societies are viewed as structured on a number of factors—age, gender, race, and social class, to name a few. Let's look at an example.

Activity

While sociologists are quick to admit that an individual's action at the micro level relies on a measure of personal choice, we also hold that large portions of these choices are structured in and can be attributed to larger social structures. Go to **http://www.cdc.gov/nchs/**

1. Who runs this site?

2. Click on "FASTSTATS A TO Z" in the column on the left to see the wide range of topics covered by this agency.

3. Now go to **http://www.cdc.gov/nchs/faststats/pdf/hus99t61.pdf**

4. How do race, age and gender appear to impact the use of tobacco?

5. What changes in tobacco use do you see in the United States over the time frames presented?

6. What other variables might account for the patterned use of tobacco?

Social Structure 2

Overview

Using the concept of social structure can be empowering. In fact, implementing structure can be a valuable applied skill. While the structure is often viewed at a macro level, it has great importance at the "meso" or middle level as well. Let's look.

Activity

Let's first turn to an example of an effort to structure a work environment. Go to **http://www.itd.emory.edu/ITD/Design/**

1. Who runs this site?

2. Browse through some of the links on the page.

3. Did sociologists design this structure?

4. Click on "social structure" and work through the links.

5. What elements are included in this structure, that is, what things were structured?

6. What can we learn from this example?

Other Sites on Social Structure	
URL Link	**Summary: Who runs the site? Description?**

Social Interaction and Networks 1

part
2

Overview

Key to establishing relationships is social interaction. This interaction may occur in a variety of ways. Let's try our hand at some possible interactions.

Activity

Here are some sites that attempt to connect sociology students by encouraging interaction.

http://cwolf.alaska.edu/~anlmg/soc/soc.html

http://tile.net/listserv/soctalkl.html

1. What impact might these sites have on students in sociology?

2. What value do they have to you?

3. How is this interaction different than a person-to-person discussion about sociology?

Social Interaction and Networks 2

Overview

The coming of cyberspace has changed interaction. Is face-to-face interaction gone forever? What differences can we expect from social interaction on the computer versus face-to-face? Let's see.

Activity

Here is one person's view of the differences in interaction—computer versus face-to-face. Go to **http://hsb.baylor.edu/ramsower/ais.ac.96/ papers/rocco.htm**

1. What was investigated in this article?

2. What did the researcher discover?

3. Do you agree? What do you believe are the differences in these types of interactions?

Social Interaction and Networks 3

Overview

Sociologists emphasize the importance of interaction in understanding human social patterns. How does this work? How can interacting produce patterns of action? Let's look at a possible answer.

Activity

To answer this question we need to uncover a process that explains the products of interaction. Go to **http://www.runet.edu/~lridener/courses/ REALITY. HTML**

1. Read this article carefully.

2. How can human interaction produce society?

3. What theoretical perspective in sociology does this article reflect?

part

2

4. Use the process outlined in this article to explain the emergence of some everyday life situation.

5. Does it work? That is, can the situation be explained by using information from this article?

Other Sites on Social Interaction and Networks	
URL Link	**Summary: Who runs the site? Description?**

part
2

Groups 1

Overview

Sociology is the study of interactions and, hence, groups. What does this mean? We call many clusters of people "groups." Let's get a definition.

Activity

Go to **http://campus.murraystate.edu/academic/faculty/frank.elwell/ prob3/GLOSSARY/socgloss.htm** Elwell's Glossary provides some online definitions of key sociology terms. Now, find definitions for each of the following:

1. Social groups

2. Primary group

3. Primary group structure

4. Secondary group

5. Secondary group structure

Groups 2

Overview

Sometimes there's nothing like going back to the original source to clarify understanding of a topic. Let's look at what the term "primary group" was intended to mean.

Activity

Go to **http://www.runet.edu/~lridener/courses/PRIMGRP. HTML**

1. Who authored this article? When?

2. Read the article.

3. What was intended by the term "primary group?"

4. What does he mean by "primary association?"

5. Give some examples of groups and associations that fit this description.

6. Are these very useful ideas, that is, do they help you to make sense of social interaction?

Groups 3

Overview

Recently the importance of teamwork has made its way into American corporate life in the public and private sectors. Knowledge of groups that we get in sociology is a great link to understanding teams, and another reason to understand sociology. Let's look.

Activity

Go to **http://www.workteams.unt.edu/**

1. Who runs this site?

2. Browse the site. Follow some of the links.

3. What are some of the areas of interest explored here?

4. How can a general understanding of groups and interaction help you understand teams?

5. What occupations might use this skill?

Other Sites on Groups	
URL Link	**Summary: Who runs the site? Description?**

part
2

Bureaucracy and Formal Organizations 1

Overview

Business Process Reengineering has become part of daily life within organizations. What is it? Would an understanding of sociology be useful in understanding and implementing it? Let's find out.

Activity

To get an understanding of business process reengineering go to
http://www.reengineering.com/hotlinks.htm

1. Spend some time reviewing the links provided on this site.

2. Try to determine what BPR is. In your own words, what would you say BPR is?

3. Now link the sociology you have learned so far to the process of BPR. In what ways is an understanding of sociology helpful here?

Bureaucracy and Formal Organizations 2

Overview

part 2

Organizations take on many shapes and forms, or structures. Knowing the structure of an organization can be very helpful in understanding the nature of social interaction within it.

Activity

As a basic overview of organizational structure, go to **http://www. imaginiz.com/6models.html**

1. Identify and briefly describe the six models of organization presented here.

2. How would social interaction be different in each?

3. What are the strengths and weaknesses of each? Whose ideas are these anyway? Go to **http://www.yorku.ca/faculty/academic/ gmorgan/index.html**

Bureaucracy and Formal Organizations 3

Overview

Who leads a formal organization? How can an organization be led? Leaders and leadership are topics of recent concern.

Activity

How can sociologists get involved in the process of developing leaders and leadership? Go to **http://www.exen.com/**

1. What is this organization? What is its purpose?

2. Consider the concepts that you've learned so far. What does sociology as a field and/or sociologists have to bring to an organization such as the one on this site?

Other Sites on Bureaucracy and Formal Organizations	
URL Link	**Summary: Who runs the site? Description?**

part

2

Deviance and Social Control 1

Overview

Crime is often viewed as one of the most obvious forms of social deviance. Law breaking has been the target of a great amount of social resources and public concern. What is the general nature of crime?

A very interesting starting point, and a useful site, is the Bureau of Justice Statistics. BJS is a warehouse of data on crime. Let's go to **http://www.ojp.usdoj.gov/bjs/**

1. Take some time just to explore the site. Now, return to the home page and click on "search this site."

When you get to the search engine, type in "trends"

    a. Select and review the trends in crime in the United States from 1965–the most recent date in the data that have some interest to you.

    b. How would you characterize the overall trend in crime?

    c. Are there any types of crime that have varied differently than the overall trend?

    d. Use your sociological imagination: What accounts for the differences in 3 and 4 above?

part

2

Deviance and Social Control 2

Overview

Deviance and society's response to it take numerous forms across cultures. Let's look at some variations on the theme of deviance: its definition and the response to it.

Activity

For each of these links, determine:

1. How is deviance determined?

2. Who decides what is deviant?

3. What response is expected?

4. How are these similar and different?

    Go to **http://www.umm.maine.edu/BEX/SocMod/SMMod3Deviance.html** and **http://www.nwmissouri.edu/library/religion/americanreligion.html** Now, apply this conceptualization of deviance to a selection of items on this site: **http://web.mala.bc.ca/crim/dev/default.htm** (many possibilities here, choose among them).

5. Does the way one defines deviance have an impact on interpretation?

Other Sites on Deviance and Social Control	
URL Link	**Summary: Who runs the site? Description?**

Stratification 1

part
2

Overview

Most of us are aware that income and wealth are not equally distributed in the United States. But, to what extent is this the case? If income inequality does exist, so what? Does it really change the way people behave, the way they live, their opportunities? Do subcultures of people, social class subcultures, or different ways of living emerge as a result of these differences?

Activity

What is the general distribution income in families in the United States? What percent of the total income does each 20 percent, that is each fifth, of the families in the United States get? To find out, go to **www.census. gov/hhes/income/incineq/p60tb1.html**

1. Describe the distribution of income in the United States

2. With respect to income distribution, are things getting more equal or less equal overall?

3. Use a sociological perspective. How did this distribution of income get this way? Why are the categories different? What caused the differences?

4. Use your sociological imagination—What impact does this income distribution have on society?

Stratification 2

Overview

We often look at social stratification—social layering—in our local community or in our nation. Does stratification exist globally? That is, does it exist across societies? How can we find out?

Activity

part
2

Start by going to the World Bank's indicators data base at **http://www. ciesin.org/mep-bin/charlotte?state=START&event=start&protocol= sid&charlotte_dir=prod&charlotte_server=www.ciesin.org**

Now, to begin to determine if layering exists in the global village, create a table in which you compare the United Sates to three other countries (Note: this activity is not an attempt to reinforce stereotypes).

Put the following in your table:

1. One country that you believe has a standard of living similar to the United States.

2. One country that you believe has a standard of living lower than the United States, but not the lowest in the world.

3. One country that you believe has a standard of living among the lowest in the world.

4. Click on "compare only years with data," and compare these four countries (the United States and the three others) on the following indicators:

   a. Energy consumption per capita

   b. GNP per capita (US$)

   c. Illiteracy rate for the total population

    d. Life expectancy at birth for the total population

    e. Infant mortality rate

    f. Upper poverty line, headcount (percent of population)

5. Speculate from these indicators: How would life be different in each of these societies?

6. Is there reason to suggest that stratification exists globally?

Other Sites on Stratification	
URL Link	**Summary: Who runs the site? Description?**

Social Class 1

Overview

A segment of the U.S. population lives in poverty. But, what does it mean to live in poverty?

Activity

The U.S. government has adopted a measurement scheme to identify those in poverty. Let's see how this is done. Go to **http://aspe.os.dhhs. gov/poverty/97poverty.htm**

1. What characteristics does the government use to determine a level of poverty?

2. What are the strengths and weaknesses of using this measurement device to determine poverty?

3. What characteristics would you use to make this distinction?

Social Class 2

Overview

Many Americans identify with the middle class. What does this mean? Let's take a look.

Activity

part
2

The Census Bureau addresses the notion of middle class in an interesting way. Go to **http://www.census.gov/hhes/income/midclass/midclsan.html**

1. How does the Census Bureau deal with the notion of middle class and income distribution?

2. There are other ways to define class. How would you apply them here?

Other Sites on Social Class	
URL Link	**Summary: Who runs the site? Description?**

Race and Ethnicity 1

Overview

Publicly and in sociology we often discuss minority groups. What does it mean to have minority status? What impact does it have on people?

Activity

Go to **http://www.trinity.edu/~mkearl/race.html**

1. Who runs this site?

2. Read through the initial paragraphs. Keep reading until you read the discussion of minority groups.

3. What central features characterize a minority group?

4. Browse through this site and explore the links.

5. Do the racial and ethnic groups listed on this site conform to the minority group characteristics above? Which ones?

6. Must a minority group be a numerical minority? Explain your answer.

Race and Ethnicity 2

Overview

In a pluralistic culture, understanding the differences among the ways of life maintained by differing racial and ethnic groups is difficult, to say the least. Let's get some help in locating some references that compare selected racial and ethnic groups.

Activity

Go to the American Studies Web site on **http://www.georgetown.edu/ crossroads/asw/**

1. Who runs this site?

part

2

2. Spend some time just investigating the range of offerings on this page.

3. Now, click on "Race and Ethnicity."

4. Review the content of this link. Which racial and ethnic groups are identified here?

5. For each group, investigate at least one link and indicate what you found.

Other Sites on Race and Ethnicity	
URL Link	**Summary: Who runs the site? Description?**

Gender 1

Overview

The key to understanding gender differences between men and women from a sociological view is the patterned and different way that they are socialized. Are there really patterned differences?

Activity

To start, go to **http://www.academic.org/**

part

2

1. Who runs this site?

2. Browse through some of the links on the page.

3. According to those who run this site, what accounts for a large share of the differences between men and women?

4. This group recommends a change in the way we socialize girls. What are the strengths and weaknesses in things that they propose?

5. Would these proposed recommendations have an impact on boys, too? Explain.

Gender 2

Overview

Understanding changing gender roles is valuable information in understanding a changing society. Are there really issues that are gender specific? Let's consider this.

part

2

Activity

Start your search by going to **http://www.inform.umd.edu/EdRes/Topic/ WomensStudies/**

1. Who runs this site?

2. Browse through some of the links on the page.

3. Now, scroll down to "gender issues" and click.

4. What issues are suggested to be largely "gender issues?" Why are they labeled this way?

5. What impact do these issues have on women? What impact do these issues have on men?

Other Sites on Gender	
URL Link	**Summary: Who runs the site? Description?**

Age and Aging 1

Overview

We hear a great deal about the elderly population in the United States What are the characteristics of this group? Let's find out.

Activity

Let's view the segment of the population that is over 65 years of age. Go to **http://www.census.gov/socdemo/www/agebrief.html**

1. Describe the growth of this segment of the U.S. population. How will this group grow over the next 50 years?

2. What special needs will this group have as they age?

3. Will the society need to change to accommodate these needs?

4. What changes are likely?

Age and Aging 2

Overview

Taking a structural–functionalist approach, we would expect to see the emergence of an increasing number of voluntary and formal organizations in the presence of a major population change, such as the increasing number of elderly in American society. These organizations arise to meet the personal and social needs of this group. Has this happened for the elderly?

Activity

Check out the site at **http://www.aoa.dhhs.gov/aoa/resource.html**

1. Search or check the Table of Contents and review the resources listed on this site.

2. Categorize this list into 3–4 topics (such as Federal and state organizations, special needs organizations, and voluntary associations, for example).

3. Visit some of these sites in each of the categories that you've created above. For each site, indicate its purpose, the target population (the specific group it serves) and who funds it.

4. How would you characterize these resources?

Age and Aging 3

Overview

Many social forces will influence the nature of life for aging persons. What are some of these forces and how will they impact the lives of this group?

Activity

Review the site at **http://pr.aoa.dhhs.gov/aoa/stats/aging21**

part

2

1. Who wrote this article?

2. What are the four major categories of forces that will likely shape the lives of the elderly in the next century?

3. For each category, click on the link and review the social forces that are identified. Briefly note the impact that each is expected to have.

4. How would you summarize the life of the elderly in the next century?

Other Sites on Age and Aging	
URL Link	**Summary: Who runs the site? Description?**

part
2

Health 1

Overview

Where could you go if you wanted to investigate health and wellness globally and within the United States? While you could search state-by-state, you might start at a central source. Let's look at some of these sources.

Activity

Let's start by looking globally. Go to **http://www.who.ch**

1. Who runs this site?

2. Click on search, and then search for a health related issue or illness.

3. What did you find? Are there any language barriers?

Now let's turn to the United States. Go to **http://www.cdc.gov**

1. Who runs this site?

2. Click on search, and then search for the same health related issue or illness that you investigated above.

3. What did you find?

4. Stop by the employment section and see if there are any interesting jobs.

Another source that might be interesting could be found at **http://www.cdc.gov/nchswww**

1. Who runs this site?

2. Click on NCHS Web Search, and then search for the same health related issue or illness that you investigated above.

3. What do you notice about this search site?

part

2

Health 2

Overview

How healthy is our society? How would we know? The need to understand the general health and wellness of a nation or a society is an important sociological focus. Let's take a look.

Activity

To start your briefing today, let's go to the White House. Go to **http://www.whitehouse.gov/fsbr/ssbr.html**

1. Now, click on "Health."

2. What are the indicators that are measured on this site?

3. Review each graph and accompanying data.

4. Summarize the information for each (What is happening?).

5. How would you characterize this method of measuring health in a society?

Health 3

Overview

Do you or your family have health insurance? If your answer is no, you know the concern you face when you need to have even basic health needs met. Healthy people have better chances of achieving their goals in life. But, is this access equal? Does everyone have the same chance to have some or all of their medical and health needs paid for by insurance? This Internet activity looks at stratification as a force in the access to health care.

part
2

Activity

Start your investigation by going to **http://www.census.gov/hhes/ hlthins/cover95/c95taba.html**

1. What is the general distribution of health insurance in the United States? How many people have it, and what kind do they have? How many people have it and how many don't have it?

2. What are the major sources of health insurance?

3. Now go to **http://www.census.gov/hhes/hlthins/cover95/c95tabb. html**

4. What factors influence the access to health insurance?

5. What are the differences?

6. Use your sociological imagination—What impact would these differences (if they exist) have on society?

Other Sites on Health	
URL Link	**Summary: Who runs the site? Description?**

 Education 1

Overview

Monitoring the educational well-being of a society is essential. Cross cultural and internal comparisons on just how well we're doing are often made by parents, teachers, politicians and individuals from all walks of life. Let's investigate some education indicators in the United States.

Activity

To start your briefing today, let's go to the White House. Go to **http://www.whitehouse.gov/fsbr/ssbr.html**

1. Now, click on "Education."

2. Name the indicators that are measured on this site?

3. Review each graph and accompanying data.

4. Summarize the information for each (What is happening?).

5. How would you characterize this method of measuring education in a society?

Education 2

Overview

The impact of the Internet on education will continue to challenge the way we learn. Let's look at some of the courses that are available in higher education.

Activity

Today you'll enter a different lecture hall. Go to **http://www.utexas.edu/world/lecture/** and/or **http://www.mcli.dist.maricopa.edu/tl/**

1. Use the search engine at this site to explore some of the courses that you are currently taking or might like to take. Type in the key word of the course you're interested in and see what happens.

2. Enter one of the courses that you have found. What is your assessment of the course at this site?

3. What impact will this type of learning have on education in the United States? What impact will it have globally? What impact will it have on you?

Education 3

Overview

Where can you get a good start when you're looking for data on education in the United States? Let's take a look at one clearinghouse for U.S. data on education.

Activity

On our review of education, start by going to **http://nces.ed.gov/**

1. Who runs this site?

2. Click on "Data and Surveys." Now review the list of research projects underway. Note that in most cases the results are not

available. Rather, these are reviews of research and research design. How would you characterize the extent of the projects as presented here?

3. Now use the search engine on this site: **http://nces.ed.gov/search.html**

4. Use the search engine at this site to explore some areas of interest. Start by typing "sociology."

5. Explore some of the data and data tables that are listed.

6. Identify and write a brief summary of the findings in a table of your choice.

Education 4

Overview

What is the nature of American education? Sometimes, amid the claims and controversy, it is difficult to know for sure. Let's take a look at U.S. education at three different levels.

part
2

Activity

1. Return to the National Center for Education and use their search engine at **http://nces.ed.gov/search.html**

2. Now type "elementary education." Search and browse through the information that emerges. Now, select one data source and summarize what you found.

3. Now type "secondary education." Search and browse through the information that emerges. Now, select one data source and summarize what you found.

4. Now type "postsecondary education." Search and browse through the information that emerges. Now, select one data source and summarize what you found.

Other Sites on Education	
URL Link	**Summary: Who runs the site? Description?**

Family 1

Overview

Two-career families and the changing nature of the way we raise children in the United States have had many impacts. Did you ever wonder what do school-age children do with their time? Let's find out.

Activity

Explore the Fact Sheet on School-Age Children from the National Institute on Out-of-School Time at the Center for Research on Women, Wellesley College at **http://www.wellesley.edu/WCW/CRW/SAC/ factsht.html**

1. How do school age children generally spend their time?

2. Why should anyone be concerned about this?

3. What problems or issues are associated with the use of time by school-age children?

Family 2

Overview

Single parent families are a part of family life in the United Sates. How prevalent is this form of family structure? What impact has it had on the way we raise children?

Activity

Interpret the information in the following table on this link:
http://nces.ed.gov/pubs/yi/y9611a.html

This graph represents the data in the table above: **http://nces.ed.gov/pubs/yi/y9611c.html**

1. How does single parent familihood vary according to this graph?

2. How would you describe the prevalence of single parent families in the United States?

3. What impact, if any, has this had on early socialization?

part

2

Other Sites on Family	
URL Link	**Summary: Who runs the site? Description?**

Economy 1

Overview

Like many societal level or macro level characteristics, national economy is often measured using indicators. Indicators are measures that stand for something that is happening. Let's look at some indicators of the U.S. economy.

Activity

First list the indicators provided in the site **http://www.census.gov/ briefrm/esbr/www/brief.html**

1. For each indicator, determine the direction the indicator is going. Is it basically going up, down or remaining the same over the time period provided?

2. Using the graphics, look for associations between the indicators. That is, as one indicator appears to be going up, what is happening to another indicator?

3. What useful information can sociology add to this type of analysis?

Economy 2

Overview

Consider the impact of labor unions on your standard of living. Labor unions have had a large impact not only on American economy, but also on our lifestyle. Let's see if we can get a sense of this impact.

Activity

Go to and review **http://www.igc.org/igc/labornet/**

1. List the topics that appear to be of interest to labor union members on this page.

part

2

2. Select 2–3 of these topics and follow their links. Briefly describe what you found in each.

3. Why do you believe that these topics were viewed as valuable?

Economy 3

Overview

Economic Institutions: What Does the Job Situation Look Like? No doubt, one of the key reasons you're in college is to find a good job. Don't forget that jobs are roles—sets of expectations and obligations for human action. As such, they are connected to the economic institution which is affected by all other social institutions and societal forces. In order to improve your chances in the job search, it would be wise to investigate the direction society and the economic institution is headed. Let's do this.

Activity

1. What will tomorrow's jobs look like? Let's find out by going to **http://stats.bls.gov/oco/oco2003.htm**

2. Who runs this site?

3. What is likely to occur with regard to employment growth between now and 2005?

4. What social forces are responsible for this change?

5. How might this change affect you?

Economy 4

Overview

Businesses and consumer groups actively use social science methods to track consumers. In many ways, this is a direct application of sociological perspectives and methods. Let's review an example of a business-oriented look at social patterns.

part
2

Activity

To start our search, go to **http://www.demographics.com/**

1. Once you're there, click on "American Demographics: Consumer trends for business leaders."

2. Now, click on one of the articles.

3. How was a sociological perspective used in this article?

4. Now, search some of the back issues. Scan 3–5 articles.

5. In general, how could sociology add value to the information presented?

<table>
<tr><td colspan="2">Other Sites on Economy</td></tr>
<tr><td>URL Link</td><td>Summary: Who runs the site? Description?</td></tr>
<tr><td></td><td></td></tr>
<tr><td></td><td></td></tr>
<tr><td></td><td></td></tr>
</table>

part

2

Religion 1

Overview

Sociology can be valuable in simply appreciating the breadth of religious beliefs in a society or cross-culturally. How many religious groups can you name? What do members of each group believe?

Activity

1. List the religious groups that you can think of right now. Take a few minutes with this.

2. Now go to **http://weber.u.washington.edu/~madin/**

3. Browse through the site. Compare this list with yours. Any additions needed?

4. Now search the links for the religions that were originally in your list (the ones you knew about before this activity). Jot down anything new that you might discover.

5. Now pick 1–3 religions that you either had not heard of or whose beliefs you were uncertain about. What did you discover?

6. Use your sociological imagination: What impact does religion have on human social life?

Religion 2

Overview

Can a religious movement be a social movement? What is the breadth of religious movements? Let's find out.

Activity

1. Now go to **http://cti.itc.virginia.edu/~jkh8x/soc257/profiles.html**

2. Who runs this site?

3. These profiles seek to look at a variety of religious movements.

4. Scroll down the page and select 3–5 of these groups.

5. Compare and contrast them (their profile and beliefs).

   How does this variety of religious belief impact society?

Other Sites on Religion	
URL Link	**Summary: Who runs the site? Description?**

Politics 1

Overview

Political changes are fast breaking and are often difficult to monitor. They occur at each level of society: macro, middle range and micro. Let's see if we can grasp the range and the organization of political activity in the United States.

Activity

To start our tour of political structure, go to **http://www.politicalindex.com**

1. Who runs this site?

2. Now, investigate this site—click on areas of interest that span different levels of social organization: national/international, state and local.

3. Identify and briefly discuss what you found at each of these levels.

4. Pick some areas that look like they would be fun. What are they? What did you discover?

5. How does your understanding of sociology help you understand these political elements of our society?

Politics 2

Overview

Much of what we learn about politics is transmitted by the news media. Are the stories the same from newspaper to newspaper or television news station to news station? Let's see.

Activity

Many television network news services put their information on the Internet. Here are three different Internet sites:

http://www.abcnews.com/

http://www.nbcnews.com/news/default.asp

http://www.cbs.com/navbar/news.html

part **2**

Find a national or international level political story that appears on this service. Read the story and outline it. Pay attention to the way the story is presented. Now go to the remaining links. For each one:

1. Determine if the story appears on the link.

2. If it does appear, compare and contrast it with the way the other stories were presented.

3. Do this for each of the remaining links.

4. Now, how were these news reports similar and different? If you found a difference, speculate as to why this might be so.

Other Sites on Politics	
URL Link	**Summary: Who runs the site? Description?**

Population 1

Overview

Understanding human population—how many, what kind, and how fast it is growing—is an essential sociological tool. Let's get a general sense of some of the dimensions of human population.

Activity

Go to the Population Reference Bureau's site at **http://www.prb.org/prb/**

1. Spend some time reviewing the links on the site.

2. Now try your hand at playing the Demographic Challenge Game by clicking the oval around the middle of the Bureau's home page. How did you do?

Population 2

Overview

Census data are valuable in understanding the past, present and future transitions in population. The U.S. Bureau of Census maintains a vast storehouse of data.

Activity

Go to **http://www.census.gov/**

1. For fun, click on the "Census Clock," the Current U.S. Population Count. How many people are in the U.S. population? (Indicate the time and date, too.)

2. Go back to the "Clock" 2 minutes later. What is the population now?

3. How did they do that?

4. Now click on "Search," and go to the Census search function.

5. Type in some key words or click on the first letter of a key word for which you would like some population information.

6. What did you find?

Other Sites on Population	
URL Link	**Summary: Who runs the site? Description?**

part

2

Urbanization and Community 1

Overview

Community can appear in a variety of environments. We often think about rural and urban communities within human societies, but let's turn to an emerging area in which community may reside.

Activity

As a contractor for NASA you have been asked (because of your socio-logical background, of course) to advise the agency director on the basic factors that NASA should address when considering the development of space communities. Go to **http://science.nas.nasa.gov/Services/ Education/SpaceSettlement/index.html**

1. What factors would influence development of space communities?

2. How would space communities likely be different than Earth communities? How would they be similar?

3. Identify 3–5 critical areas to which the agency director should address her attention.

Urbanization and Community 2

part 2

Overview

Most of us would agree that life in cities is different than suburban or rural living. How is the size of a city associated with certain quality of life indicators? Let's find out.

Activity

1. How do the 25 cities with the largest population rank with regard to crime and infant mortality?

2. Access **http://www.census.gov/statab/ccdb/ccdb309.txt** with your browser.

Now, draw two graphs. On one, plot the rankings of city size on the x axis and the rank for the crimes/100,000 on the y axis. (When cities share the same rank, the next lower rank is omitted. CDP = census designated place.) Draw in a best-fitting straight line. On the second one, plot the rankings of city size on the x axis and infant death rates/1000 live births on the y axis. Draw in a best-fitting straight line for each graph.

1. Go to **http://www.census.gov/statab/ccdb/ccdb310.txt** and create two more graphs (repeat the procedure in #2 above) for the ranking of percent of elementary and high school enrollments and percent bachelor's degrees.

2. What did you discover? What associations did you find?

3. Use your sociological imagination—Why did this happen?

4. What other variables might influence the outcomes?

Urbanization and Community 3

Overview

While urbanization and its impact are important, we may neglect issues that face rural and agriculturally oriented communities. Take some time to investigate some of these issues in the United States and around the world.

Activity

Agricultural interests are often intertwined with rural interests. In our first step to investigate these interests, go to **http://www.card.iastate.edu**

1. Who runs this site? Why do you think this group maintains it?

2. Browse through the site.

3. Click on "emerging issues." Now, categorize the types of issues that you find here.

4. For this one point in time, what seem to be the issues of importance?

5. Click on some links that are most interesting to you? What are they? Why are they interesting?

6. How can sociology be used to understand these issues?

part
2

Other Sites on Urbanization and Community	
URL Link	**Summary: Who runs the site? Description?**

Environment 1

Overview

Have you been hungry today? Food production is a good example of the interaction between human social systems and the environment. Let's look at attempts to monitor this interaction globally.

Activity

This site attempts to provide an early warning system on global food shortages. Go to **http://www.fao.org/WAICENT/faoinfo/economic/ giews/giewse.htm**

1. Who runs this site?

2. Browse through the site.

3. Review the Food Outlook for the most recent report. Click on "Highlights."

4. What is the status of food availability?

5. Use your sociological imagination: In this interaction between human societies and environment, what social forces and natural forces influence the availability of food?

Environment 2

Overview

Human societies interact with the environment in countless ways. What are some of the outcomes of this interaction? Let's look at a list of possibilities.

Activity

Go to **http://www.ulb.ac.be/ceese/cds.html**

1. Who runs this site?

2. Browse through the list of issues and ideas on this site.

3. Select 2–3 of interest to you.

4. Now, for each item that you have selected consider the nature of the interaction of humans and the environment.

5. Take a systems (functionalist or ecological) point of view. Interpret your findings above. Now take a conflict view. How would you interpret these differently?

part
2

Environment 3

Overview

What action is taking place to deal with society's impact on environment? Let's take a walk around our environment and find out.

Activity

Go to **http://www.envirolink.org/EnviroLink_Library/**

1. Who runs this site?

2. Now take a walk around by clicking on water, air and the other icons presented.

3. Using your sociological perspective, how would you characterize the kinds of action listed here?

4. What forces in society are working for and against these activities?

Other Sites on Environment	
URL Link	**Summary: Who runs the site? Description?**

Technology 1

Overview

What is "technology?" This term is often used. How does it relate to social change and changing human life? Let's investigate.

Activity

First define *technology.*

1. Either look for the term in a sociology textbook or go to **http://campus.murraystate.edu/academic/faculty/frank.elwell/prob3/GLOSSARY/socgloss.htm**

2. Now, go to **http://www.ctheory.com/**

3. What is presented on this site?

4. Browse through the site and choose 2–3 articles that might interest you.

5. In each article identify the technological factor(s) that is operating, and then describe that factor's impact on society as portrayed in the article.

Technology 2

Overview

The diffusion of new technology is often uneven. That is, it doesn't get to everybody at the same time. Some groups get it faster than others do. There are many factors that influence this diffusion. Let's look at an attempt to address these factors.

Activity

Go to **http://arachne.cns.iit.edu/~livewire/**

1. Who runs this site?

2. Click on "general information." What is this site intended to do?

Just looking at the information on this site, what social factors that may influence the diffusion of technology are addressed on this site?

part

2

Other Sites on Technology	
URL Link	**Summary: Who runs the site? Description?**

Collective Behavior 1

Overview

Public opinion is of concern to sociologists in general and those who study collective behavior specifically. An understanding of the collective perspective of a public can be a powerful tool.

Activity

Many organizations are involved locally, nationally and internationally in assessing public opinion. They view opinions at a variety of levels. Review public opinion at three different levels of social organization by going to these sites:

part
2

> U.S. and International: **http://www.gallup.com/**
>
> Primarily United States: **http://www.isr.umich.edu/src/projects.html** (Click on some of the SRC projects of interest to you)
>
> **http://www.icpsr.umich.edu/gss/home.htm** (Click on "Trends in GSS Variables" and the "GSS Search Engine")
>
> Local Research Examples: **http://sluweb.selu.edu/Academics/Depts/fpssrc/**
>
> **http://www.aacc.cc.md.us/ddnataf/csli.html** (Click on "Surveys of . . .)

1. Who runs these sites?

2. Review sample research (if available) on each site.

3. How can these data be used?

4. What are the strengths and weaknesses of collecting and using public opinion data?

Collective Behavior 2

Overview

What are social movements? We hear about them often. Let's take a look.

Activity

Go to **http://www.asanet.org/sections/collect.html** This is the section on Collective Behavior and Social Movements of the American Sociological Association.

1. Under the Welcome you'll find a description of just what is studied by persons who research social movements.

2. Given the information in #1, how would you define a social movement?

3. Now visit the following site: **http://www.wsu.edu:8080/~amerstu/ smc/smcframe.html**

4. Browse some of the links on social movements.

5. What are the similarities and differences among these groups?

Other Sites on Collective Behavior	
URL Link	**Summary: Who runs the site? Description?**

part

2

Social Movements 1

Overview

People often organize and change the course of an ongoing social system. When this happens we witness the emergence of a social movement.

Do you see such movements around you in our society? What types of movements are emerging? Are they occurring globally? Let's look.

Activity

First, go to **http://www.stile.lut.ac.uk/~gyobs/GLOBAL/t0000006.html**

1. Who runs this site?

2. Browse through the list of categories of social movements.

3. Select 2–3 of these category areas that are of interest to you.

4. What are some of the movements emerging in each category?

Now, go to **http://www.stile.lut.ac.uk/~gyobs/GLOBAL/t0000006.html**

1. Browse through the list of areas on this site.

2. Select 2–3 geographic areas that are of interest to you.

3. What movements are emerging in these locations?

4. What impact does the presence of these social movements have on living in this society?

Social Movements 2

Overview

Social movements may exist at a variety of levels. Concern for changing some aspect of the social condition may exist next door, in your country, or around the world. Let's work through an example.

Activity

Go to **http://www.brown.edu/Departments/World_Hunger_Program/ hungerweb/researchers.html**

1. Who runs this site?

2. Browse through the site. What problem is investigated here?

3. After reviewing some of the links at this site, go to **http://www.thp. org/thp/**

4. What does this group do?

5. At what levels (globally, nationally locally?) does it operate?

6. Now go to **http://www.action.org/**

7. What does this group do?

8. At what levels (globally, nationally locally?) does it operate?

Do these sites suggest the existence of a social movement? What is it? Use your sociological imagination: How effective is it? What social forces stand in its way?

Other Sites on Social Movements	
URL Link	**Summary: Who runs the site? Description?**

part

2

Social Change 1

Overview

Studying social change and its impact on humans and human societies is central to sociology. Change can come from many directions. Let's look at a change and speculate as to its likely impact.

Activity

Starting with the cloning of sheep, then cattle, then . . . ? Go to **http://www.pathfinder.com/@@oyHDpwcAyfO3iRGU/time/cloning/** Follow the arrows through the website.

1. What is your personal reaction to cloning?

2. What impact will cloning have on society?

3. What direct and indirect effects are likely to occur as a result of this scientific breakthrough?

Social Change 2

Overview

Social change does not always occur at the macro or societal level. Many organizations—business, government, health care, education, and religious groups—attempt to anticipate and manage the change process. An applied sociologist engaging in sociological practice must not only learn the concepts and perspectives of sociology, but also those of the clients she may engage. One of the models for handling change is the continuous improvement model. Let's investigate this model.

Activity

Go to **http://www.westvirginia.com/www/trev/mts/Contimp.htm** Now, spend some time investigating the various aspects of the continuous improvement process.

1. How is this process similar to the perspectives and process you have learned while studying sociology?

2. What concepts in sociology would help you more effectively assist a client in utilizing this process in her organization?

Social Change 3

Overview

Increasingly, we have needed to reflect on the direct impact of societies beyond our own. This globalization of our view has been a source of social change.

Activity

Review this overview of a recent PBS special on globalization. Go to
http://www.pbs.org/globalization/home.html

1. Review the summary of change and globalization. Do the makers of this site view globalization as having a positive or negative effect on other countries?

2. What changes have occurred in the U.S. and abroad as a result of globalization?

3. At what levels within the business world have these changes occurred?

Other Sites on Social Change	
URL Link	**Summary: Who runs the site? Description?**

part
2

The Future of Society 1

Overview

Analyzing trends, patterned and emerging changes, in society may give us some clues as to the society in which we are likely to find ourselves in the future. How could something that is likely to be happening in the future be realistically used in the present? Let's see.

Activity

Review this company report on the use of trend research to influence company focus. Go to **http://www.acm.org/sigs/sigchi/chi97/proceedings/briefing/rl.htm**

1. Read the report.

2. What trends did this company recognize that its leadership believed would have an impact on its product lines?

3. What was the actual process that the company used to brainstorm these trends and produce outcomes?

4. What did this company actually change or invent in response to the trends they identified?

The Future of Society 2

part
2

Overview

When people look into the near future, what do they see and how accurately do they see it? Let's look at one sociologist's attempt to characterize an emerging society.

Activity

Start this activity by going to **http://www.pscw.uva.nl/sociosite/TOPICS/Sociologists.html** At this site, click on "Bell, D."

1. Before you click on this article look at the Daniel Bell citation. When was this book (from which this section was derived) written?

2. Read the article.

3. How did Bell characterize the development of human societies over time; that is, what were the different societal types and how did life differ?

4. Has Bell's notion of the post-industrial society actually happened? Why do you think so?

5. What do you believe will happen after the post-industrial society?

The Future of Society 3

Overview

Many sociologists and futurists alike point to the "globalization of human action." The existence of a global social system is apparent. How aware are you of daily events around the world? Let's take a quick global tour.

Activity

Go to this site **http://www.mediainfo.com/emedia/**

1. Who runs this site?

2. To make comparison easier, select "Newspaper."

3. Now pick one newspaper from each geographic area listed. For each:

    a. What is the name of the newspaper on this site?

    b. Browse the site.

    c. What were the top news stories today?

4. Now compare and contrast the stories. What are the similarities and differences across societies in today's news?

5. What impact does the ability to collect and compare these news stories have on your view of the world?

6. Suppose that you plan to travel to this site (in person). Would this information help you?

part

2

Other Sites on The Future of Society	
URL Link	**Summary: Who runs the site? Description?**

Getting a Job with a Sociology Degree 1

Overview

Students graduating from college with a bachelor's degree in sociology may well ask: "What can I do with this degree anyway?" No doubt, you're asking this question regardless of your major in college. BA level sociology graduates have a great deal in common with other BA graduates. In many respects, job seeking and self-presentation skills are essential.

Activity

Sociologist Erving Goffman reminded us that we are constantly "presenting ourselves in everyday life." When looking for a job, this presentation can be critical. Go to **http://www.Careercity.com/**

On this site do the following:

1. How should someone dress for a job interview?

2. Construct a resume that integrates your current skills.

3. Write a short cover letter to your résumé.

4. Review the process for an electronic résumé.

5. What tips are provided for women looking for jobs?

Getting a Job with a Sociology Degree 2

Overview

Use your sociological skills to help you find a job, or at least shed some light on careers of interest to you. Let's examine some applications of sociological strategies to the job search process, and then some jobs that might be available.

Activity

1. First check out Catherine Mobley's "A Checklist for Job Hunting and Launching a Career in Applied Sociology" on **http://www.appliedsoc.org/job.htm**

2. Work through some of her suggestions for strategies to get a job.

Having completed this list, go to **http://www.politicalindex.com/sect23.htm**

1. Investigate the jobs in the various categories on this site.

2. Locate some jobs that might be interesting to you.

3. How would you apply Mobley's strategies to finding a job like those that you have found?

part

2

Other Sites on Getting a Job with a Sociology Degree	
URL Link	**Summary: Who runs the site? Description?**

New Topic:	
URL Link	**Summary: Who runs the site? Description?**

New Topic:	
URL Link	**Summary: Who runs the site? Description?**

New Topic:	
URL Link	**Summary: Who runs the site? Description?**

World Wide Web Resources for Sociologists

URLs frequently change or disappear. If you can't find a site, use one of the search engines listed below to look for it by name.

General Useful Sites

American Studies Web

http://www.georgetown.edu/crossroads/asw

Elwell's Glossary

http://campus.murraystate.edu/academic/faculty/
frank.elwell/prob3/GLOSSARY/socgloss.htm

HTML Reference Manual

http://www.sandia.gov/sci_compute/html_ref.html

Internet Resources for Sociology Students

http://www.xu.edu/depts/socdept/resources.html

Library of Congress

http://www.loc.gov

Links to Electronic Journals

http://www.edoc.com/ejournal

part
2

Sociology and Other College Courses on the Internet

Maricopa

http://www.mcli.dist.maricopa.edu/tl/

SOCNET: Sociology Courses and Curricular Resources

http://www.mcmaster.ca/socscidocs/w3virtsoclib/
socnet.htm

World Lecture Hall

http://www.utexas.edu/world/lecture/

Search Engines

AltaVista Search

http://www.altavista.digital.com

Excite Netsearch

http://www.excite.com

Lycos Search

http://www.lycos.com

WebCrawler Search

http://webcrawler.com

Yahoo! Search

http://www.yahoo.com/search.html

General Sociology Sites

American Sociological Association

http://www.asanet.org

BUBL Links: Sociology

http://link.bubl.ac.uk/sociology

Clearinghouse: Social Sciences and Social Issues

http://www.clearinghouse.net/

Electronic Journal of Sociology

http://www.sociology.org/

Galaxy Guide to Sociology

http://www.einet.net/galaxy/Social-Sciences/
Sociology.html

International Sociological Association

http://www.ucm.es/OTROS/isa

Julian Dierkes' Sociology Links at Princeton

http://www.princeton.edu/~sociolog/links.html

McGraw Hill's Social Science Web Resources

http://www.mhhe.com/socscience/sociology/

Social Science Ready Reference

http://www.mnsfld.edu/depts/lib/mu-scref.html

Sociological Abstracts Home Page

http://www.socabs.org

Sociological Tour of Cyberspace

http://www.trinity.edu/~mkearl/index.html

Sociology Courses on the Internet

http://www.mcmaster.ca/socscidocs/socnet.htm

Sociology Listservs

http://www.acs.ryerson.ca/soc/listserv.html

part
2

Sociology Places to Explore

```
http://hakatai.mcli.dist.maricopa.edu/smc/ml/
sociology.html
```

Sociology Weblinks at the University of Southern Indiana (USI)

```
http://www.usi.edu/libarts/socio/sd_wblnk.htm
```

SocioSite: Sociology in the Netherlands

```
http://www.pscw.uva.nl/sociosite
```

SOSIG: Social Science Information Gateway

```
http://sosig.esrc.bris.ac.uk
```

Progressive Sociologists Network

```
http://csf.colorado.edu/psn/
```

U. C. Berkeley Libraries: Government and Social Science Information

```
http://www.lib.berkeley.edu/GSSI/sociolog.html
```

U. Colorado's WWW Resources for Sociologists

```
http://socsci.colorado.edu/SOC/RES
```

U. Missouri-St. Louis Sociology Links

```
http://www.umsl.edu/~sociolog/resource.htm
```

Western Connecticut State University's Sociology Internet Resources

```
http://www.wcsu.ctstateu.edu/socialsci/socres.html
```

WWW Virtual Library: U.S. Government Information Sources

```
http://iridium.nttc.edu/gov_res.html
```

Yahoo!: Sociology

```
http://www.yahoo.com/Social_Science/Sociology
```

Aging

The AARP Guide to Internet Resources Related to Aging

http://www.aarp.org/cyber/guide1.htm

Administration on Aging

http://www.aoa.dhhs.gov

On-Line Periodicals on Aging

http://www.usc.edu/isd/elecresources/subject/
social_Geront.html

AOA Directory of WEB and Gopher Sites on Aging

http://www.aoa.dhhs.gov/aoa/webres/craig.htm

AOA Internet and Email Resources on Aging

http://www.aoa.dhhs.gov/aoa/pages/jpostlst.html

Clifton E. Barber's Links to Web Sites on Aging and Gerontology

http://lamar.colostate.edu/~barberhd/links.htm

Institute for Human Development, Life Course and Aging

http://library.utoronto.ca/www/aging/depthome.html

Geriatrics Links

http://www.medwebplus.com/subject/Geriatrics.html

National Institute on Aging

http://www.nih.gov/nia/

National Council on the Aging

http://www.ncoa.org/

Recent Developments in Age Discrimination Law

http://www.lawinfo.com/forum/age.html

part
2

Social Gerontology and the Aging Revolution

`http://WWW.Trinity.Edu/~mkearl/geron.html`

U. Georgia Gerontology Center Aging Related Web Sites

`http://www.geron.uga.edu/agesites.html`

Web and Gopher Sites on Aging

`http://www.aoa.dhhs.gov/aoa/webres/craig.htm`

Applied Sociology

American Sociological Association Section on Sociological Practice

`http://www.asanet.org/sections/sphome.html`

Evaluation Review: Journal of Applied Social Research

`http://www.stat.ucla.edu/journals/er`

Keith Appleby's Research Resources in Social Science

`http://www.researchresources.net/socio.htm`

Society for Applied Sociology

`http://www.appliedsoc.org/`

Sociological Research Online

`http://kennedy.soc.surrey.ac.uk/socresonline`

Applied Tools

American Evaluation Association

`http://www.eval.org/index.html`

Business Process Reengineering and Innovation

`http://www.brint.com/BPR.htm`

Coopers & Lybrand: Government Consulting–Strategic Planning

`http://www.colybrand.com/clc/gov/stratpln.html`

Creative Problem Solving

`http://www.changedynamics.com/samples/ probsolv.htm`

Creative Problem Solving Templates

`http://www.changedynamics.com/samples/samples.htm`

Enterprise Reengineering

`http://www.reengineering.com/`

High Performance Team

`http://rampages.onramp.net/~bodwell/home.htm`

Resources for Qualitative Research

`http://www.siu.edu/~hawkes/methods. html#qualitative`

Self Directed Work Team (SDWT)

`http://users.ids.net/~brim/sdwth.html`

Steele's Quantitative and Qualitative Tool Shed

`http://www.clark.net/pub/ssteele/home.htm`

Teams and Work Teams

`http://www.workteams.unt.edu/`

World Future Society

`http://www.wfs.org/wfs/index.htm`

part

2

Collective Behavior and Social Movements

ASA Section on Collective Behavior and Social Movements

http://www.asanet.org/sections/collect.html

Ex-Cult.org

http://www.ex-cult.org/

Global Observatory's Resource Information: Social Movements of Indigenous Peoples

http://www.stile.lut.ac.uk/~gyobs/GLOBAL/
t0000087.html

Information on Militias (Links)

http://www.well.com/user/srhodes/militia.html

Neo-Militia Links Page

http://www.militia-watchdog.org/m1.htm

Pressure Groups/Interest Groups/Social Movements

http://www.library.ubc.ca/poli/cpwebint.html

Theories of Social Movements and their Current Development in Soviet Society

http://lucy.ukc.ac.uk/csacpub/russian/mamay.html

Activist Groups

Cures Not Wars Online

http://www.cures-not-wars.org

Families Against Mandatory Minimums

http://www.famm.org

Good Groups: Fighting for Justice Activist Groups

http://www.uaw.org/internet/acgroups.html

Institute for Global Communication's Communities of Activists and Organizations

http://www.igc.org/igc

Mama Gaia Ecoware's Library of Environmental Activist Groups

http://www.mamagaia.com/ecogroupsa-1.htm

No Compromise's Activist Links

http://www.enviroweb.org/nocompromise/links/index.html

Criminology, Deviance, and Criminal Justice

part **2**

Academy of Criminal Justice Sciences

http://www.acjs.org/

Access to Justice Network (Canadian)

http://www.acjnet.org

American Bar Association

http://www.abanet.org

American Correctional Association

http://www.corrections.com/aca/

American Society of Criminology

http://www.asc41.com/

Bureau of Justice Statistics

http://www.ojp.usdoj.gov/bjs

Canadian Centre on Substance Abuse

http://www.ccsa.ca

Court TV Online

http://www.courttv.com

The Critical Criminology Division of the American Society of Criminology

http://sun.soci.niu.edu/~critcrim

Drug Reform Coordination Network

http://www.drcnet.org

International Legal Resource Guide

http://www.ilrg.com

Justice Information Center

http://www.ncjrs.org

Life Education Network: Links on Drugs, Violence and AIDS Prevention

http://www.lec.org

National Institute on Drug Abuse (NIDA)

http://www.nida.nih.gov/NIDAHome.html

National Institute of Justice (UNOJUST)

http://www.ncjrs.org/unojust

National Victim Center

http://www.nvc.org

PAVNET: Partners Against Violence Network

www.pavnet.org

Prevention Online (Prevline)

http://www.health.org

part

2

SAMHSA 1995 National Household Drug Abuse Survey

http://www.health.org/pubs/95hhs/ar18txt.htm

Study Web: Criminology

http://www.studyweb.com/criminal/toc.htm

United States Parole Commission

http://www.usdoj.gov/uspc/overview.htm

Yahoo!: Crime

http://www.yahoo.com/society_and_culture/crime

Juvenile Delinquency

Juvenile Justice WWW Sites

http://www.ncjrs.org/jjwww.htm

Office of Juvenile Justice and Delinquency Prevention

http://ojjdp.ncjrs.org/

Resources for Working with At Risk Youth

http://www.monterey.edu/academic/centers/iccs/
community/atriskyouth/index.html

Vision Quest Program for At-Risk Youth

http://www.vq.com/

Culture

ASA Sociology of Culture Section

http://www.asanet.org/sections/culture.html

Chinese Historical and Cultural Project

http://www.dnai.com:80/~rutledge/CHCP_home.html

Cultures of the Andes

http://www.andes.org/

Exploring Ancient World Cultures

http://eawc.evansville.edu/index.htm

French Culture

http://frenchculture.about.com/culture/frenchculture/

The Library of Congress: American Memory

http://rs6.loc.gov

Native American Arts, Humanites and Culture

http://www.tahtonka.com/

part

2

NativeWeb: Earth's Indigenous People

www.nativeweb.org

Pacific Waves: Comparing Canadian and Australian Culture

http://edward.cprost.sfu.ca/438/index.html

Russian Culture at Mining Co.

http://russianculture.miningco.com/

The Ultimate Jewish/Israel Link Launcher

http://ucsu.colorado.edu/~jsu/launcher.html

U. of Oregon Center for Asian and Pacific Studies

http://darkwing.uoregon.edu/~caps

U. of Virginia: The Multicultural Pavilion

http://curry.edschool.virginia.edu/go/multicultural

The Web of Culture

http://www.worldculture.com

Databanks and Providers

Applied Social Data Center Home Page

http://www.cwu.edu/~asdc/home.html

General Social Survey

http://www.icpsr.umich.edu/gss

The Internet Sleuth (links to 2000+ databases)

http://www.isleuth.com

UCSD Social Sciences Data Collection

http://ssdc.ucsd.edu/ssdc/catalog.html

U.S. Statistical Abstract–Census 1994

http://www.medaccess.com/census/census_s.htm

Zeus: Eurobarometer

http://zeus.mzes.uni-mannheim.de/datasets

part
2

Demography, Population, and Urbanization

American Demographics

http://www.demographics.com/

Applied Demography

http://www.prb.org/

Center for Demography and Ecology

http://www.ssc.wisc.edu/cde/

United Nation's Information on Population and Demography

http://www.library.yale.edu/un/un3b8.htm

Ciesin's US Demography

http://www.ciesin.org/datasets/us-demog/
us-demog-home.html

Intentional Communities

http://www.well.com/user/cmty

Manfred Davidmann on Community

http://www.solbaram.org/indexes/cmmuni.html

National Civic League

http://www.ncl.org/ncl

Pennsylvania State University: Population Research Institute

http://www.pop.psu.edu

Princeton University: Office of Population Research Data Archive

http://opr.princeton.edu/archive

Princeton University: Population Index on the Web

http://popindex.princeton.edu

Rural and Small Town Programme

http://www.mta.ca/rstp

Rural Sociological Society

http://www.lapop.lsu.edu/rss

Social Science Research Computing Center's Demography Research Centers and Data Sources

http://www.spc.uchicago.edu/DATALIB/datalib.
cgi?DLothweb/index

The Urban Institute

http://www.urban.org

U.S. Census Bureau

http://www.census.gov

U.S. Census Bureau: Census State Data Centers

http://www.census.gov/sdc/www

U.S. Census Data at Lawrence Berkeley National Laboratory

http://cedr.lbl.gov/mdocs/LBL_census.html

U.S. Dept. of Housing and Urban Development: Neighborhood Networks

http://www.hud.gov/nnw/nnwindex.html

U.S. Gazetteer

http://www.census.gov/cgi-bin/gazetteer

USA CityLink Home Page

http://usacitylink.com

WWW Virtual Library: Demography & Population Studies

http://coombs.anu.edu.au/ResFacilities/
DemographyPage.html

part
2

Economy

ASA Section on Organizations, Occupations, and Work

http://www.northpark.edu/acad/soc/oow/

Bureau of Labor Statistics' Economy at a Glance

http://stats.bls.gov/eag.table.html

Electronic Policy Network

http://www.epn.org

Institute of Industrial Relations

http://violet.berkeley.edu/~iir

Job Accommodation Network

http://janweb.icdi.wvu.edu

LaborNet

http://www.igc.apc.org/labornet

Legal Information Institute: Employment Discrimination Law Materials

http://www.law.cornell.edu/topics/
employment_discrimination.html

Manfred Davidmann on Economics

http://www.solbaram.org/indexes/ecnmcs.html

part

2

United Mine Workers of America

http://www.umwa.org/homepage.shtml

The Urban Institute: Widening Wage Inequality

http://www.urban.org/periodcl/prr25_1b.htm

U.S. Dept. of Agriculture: Economic Research Service

http://www.econ.ag.gov

Education

American Association of Community Colleges

http://www.aacc.nche.edu

Ask ERIC Education Information

http://ericir.syr.edu

Aspen Institute

http://www.aspeninst.org/

Cause: Managing and Using Information Resources in Higher Education

http://cause-www.colorado.edu

The Center for Education Reform

http://edreform.com

Commonwealth of Learning

http://www.col.org

Council of the Great City Schools

http://www.cgcs.org

Diversity University (MOO provider)

http://www.du.org

Education World

http://www.education-world.com/

ERIC: Urban Education Web

http://eric-web.tc.columbia.edu

Galaxy Social Science Education Resources

http://galaxy.einet.net/galaxy/Social-Sciences.html

Global Network Academy

http://www.gnacademy.org

National Education Association (NEA)

http://www.nea.org/

School District Data Book Profiles: 1989–1990

http://govinfo.kerr.orst.edu/sddb-stateis.html

School District Demographics (subscription needed)

http://www.sunspace.com

part
2

U.S. Department of Education

http://www.ed.gov

U.S. Department of Education: Online Resources

http://www.ed.gov/EdRes/EdRes.html

Yahoo!: Education

http://www.yahoo.com/Education

 ## Environment

The British Columbia Ministry of Environment, Lands and Parks

http://www.env.gov.bc.ca/

Centre for Economic and Social Studies on the Environment

http://www.ulb.ac.be:80/ceese

Ecological Society of America

http://www.sdsc.edu/ESA/ESA.htm

EcoNet

http://www.igc.org/igc/econet/index.html

EcoTrust

http://www.ecotrust.org

EnviroLink Library

http://www.envirolink.org/EnviroLink_Library

Government Information Sharing Project

http://govinfo.kerr.orst.edu

Linkages: Resources for Environment and Development Policy Makers

http://www.iisd.ca/

National Environment Trust

http://www.envirotrust.com

National Library for the Environment

http://www.cnie.org/nle/index.shtml

Solstice: Center for Renewable Energy and Sustainable Technology (CREST)

http://solstice.crest.org

Student Environmental Action Coalition

http://www.seac.org

The Water Environment Federation

http://www.wef.org/

Yahoo!: Environment and Nature Organizations

http://www.yahoo.com/Society_and_Culture/
Environment_and_Nature/Organizations

Yahoo!: Pollution Activist Groups

http://www.yahoo.com/Society_and_Culture/
Environment_and_Nature/Pollution/Activist_Groups

part
2

Ethics

Applied Ethics Resources on WWW

http://www.ethics.ubc.ca/papers/AppliedEthics.html

Institute for Global Ethics

http://www.globalethics.org/

University of Wales: Human Subjects and Research Ethics

http://www.psych.bangor.ac.uk/DeptPsych/Ethics/
HumanResearch.html

Family

DHHS Administration for Children and Families

http://www.acf.dhhs.gov

Family.com Home Page

http://family.go.com/

The Family Research Council

http://www.frc.org

Family Village Library

http://www.familyvillage.wisc.edu/library.htm

Ring of Single Parents

http://www.webring.org/cgi-bin/webring?ring=
singleparent&list

U. of Colorado's Family Sociology Resources

http://osiris.colorado.edu/SOC/RES/family.html

Gender

Above & Beyond's Gender Resources Newsletters

http://www.abmall.com/cb/tg/news.html

American Association of University Women

http://www.aauw.org/4000/extlinks.html

Feminism and Women's Resources

http://www.ibd.nrc.ca/~mansfield/feminism

Feminist Activist Resources on the Net

http://www.igc.apc.org/women/feminist.html

Feminist.Com: Resources and Links

http://www.feminist.com/reso.htm

The Feminist Majority: Internet Gateway

http://www.feminist.org/gateway/1_gatway.html

Feminists for Free Expression

http://www.well.com/user/freedom

Gay and Lesbian Anti-Defamation Links

http://www.glaad.org/glaad/electronic/links.html

Gender and the Law at the University of Dayton

http://www.udayton.edu/~gender/

Gender and Sexuality Links

http://english-server.hss.cmu.edu/Gender.html

Gender-Related Electronic Forums

http://www-unix.umbc.edu/~korenman/wmst/forums.html

Ingersoll Gender Center—Serving the Transgender Community for 21 Years

http://www.ingersollcenter.org/

National Gay & Lesbian Task Force Links

http://www.ngltf.org/ngltflink.html

National Organization of Women: Resources on the Internet

http://www.now.org/resource.html

Voice of the Shuttle: Gender Studies Page

http://humanitas.ucsb.edu/shuttle/gender.html

Women and Gender Studies Links at Louisiana State University (LSU)

http://www.lsu.edu/guests/poli/public_html/
genlinks.htm

part

2

WomensNet

http://www.voiceofwomen.com/other.html

Women's Studies/Women's Issues Resource Sites

http://www-unix.umbc.edu/~korenman/wmst/links.html

WWWomen! Search Directory for Women Online

http://www.wwwomen.com

WWW Virtual Library: Men's Issues Page

http://www.vix.com/pub/men/index.html

WWW Virtual Library: Men's Movement Organizations

http://www.vix.com/pub/men/orgs/orgs.html

Yahoo!: Gender

http://www.yahoo.com/Society_and_Culture/Gender

part
2

Medicine and Health

AIDS Treatment News Archive

http://www.immunet.org/atn

American Cancer Society: Cancer Information Resources

http://www.cancer.org/links.html

ASH Links to Smoking Related Sites

http://ash.org/otherweb/index.html

Centers for Disease Control & Prevention

http://www.cdc.gov

Department of Health and Human Services

http://www.os.dhhs.gov

HealthLinks

http://www.hslib.washington.edu

Healthy Devil On-Line Health Topics

http://gilligan.mc.duke.edu/h-devil

Medicine and Health Sources at Bridgewater State University

http://www.bridgew.edu/DEPTS/MAXWELL/medicine.htm

Medicine Online: Medical Related Sites

http://www.mol.net

Sports Medicine and Health-Related Resources at Vassar College

http://www.iberia.vassar.edu/vcl/BI/sports.html

University of Texas' Medicine and Health Resources Page

http://www.lib.utexas.edu/Libs/LSL/LifeSci/medint.html

World Health Organization

http://www.who.ch

Yahoo!: Health

http://www.yahoo.com/Health

Media

Computer Mediated Communication Magazine Index

http://www.december.com/cmc/mag

Just Think Foundation Media Links

http://www.justthink.org/justthink.html

Mass Media and Culture Resources

http://www.uark.edu/~aca/studies/mediaculture.html

part

2

The Media History Project

http://www.mediahistory.com

Media Studies Center at the Freedom Forum

http://www.freedomforum.org/whoweare/media.asp

News Media Online

http://www.feminist.org/action/1_action.html

Project Censored: News That Didn't Make the News

http://censored.sonoma.edu/ProjectCensored

Visionary Media

http://www.visionarymedia.com/

Yahoo!: News and Media

http://www.yahoo.com/News_and_Media

part 2

News Media Online

CNN Digest

http://cnn.com/DIGEST

Jerusalem Post

http://www.jpost.co.il

Mojo Wire (Mother Jones Interactive)

http://www.mojones.com

National Public Radio Online

http://www.npr.org

Newspapers On Line

http://ftp.sff.net/people/jack.haldeman/papers.htm

NY Times Fax (subscription needed)

http://nytimesfax.com

Public Broadcasting System (PBS) Online

http://www.pbs.org

Seattle Times

http://www.seatimes.com

The Times and The Sunday Times

http://www.the-times.co.uk/news/pages/home.html?000999

USA Today

http://www.usatoday.com

Politics

African National Congress Home Page

http://www.anc.org.za

Congressional Quarterly

http://www.cq.com/

Consumer Information Center

http://www.gsa.gov/staff/pa/cic

C-SPAN

http://www.c-span.org

Deep Politics

http://www.copi.com/deepbook.htm

Electronic Policy Network

http://epn.org/

League of Women Voters

```
http://www.lwv.org/
```

National Political Index

```
http://www.politicalindex.com
```

The Organization of American States

```
http://www.oas.org
```

Political Resources on the Net

```
http://www.agora.stm.it/politic
```

Politics1

```
http://www.politics1.com/
```

Project Vote Smart

```
http://www.vote-smart.org
```

Virtual Tour of the U.S. Government

```
http://www.dreamscape.com/frankvad/us-gov.html
```

Yahoo!: Politics

```
http://www.yahoo.com/Government/Politics
```

Yahoo!: Public Interest Groups

```
http://www.yahoo.com/Society_and_Culture/Organizations
```

Poverty and Homelessness

HomeAid America: Links to Homeless Information on the Internet

```
http://www.HomeAid.org/links.htm
```

HungerWeb: Researchers Entry Point

```
http://www.brown.edu/Departments/World_Hunger_Program/
hungerweb/researchers.html
```

Institute for Research on Poverty

http://www.ssc.wisc.edu/irp

International Homeless Discussion List & Archives

http://csf.colorado.edu/homeless/index.html

Joint Center for Poverty Research

http://www.jcpr.org/about.html

Michigan Program on Poverty and Social Welfare Policy

http://www.ssw.umich.edu/poverty/mission.html

National Center for Children in Poverty

http://cpmcnet.columbia.edu/dept/nccp

National Coalition for the Homeless Directories

http://nch.ari.net/direct1.html

National Coalition for the Homeless Online Library

http://nch.ari.net/database.html

National Law Center on Homelessness and Poverty

http://www.nlchp.org/

Resources for Ending Poverty and Hunger

http://action.org/resources.html

Twentieth Century Fund Brief on Welfare Reform

http://www.tcf.org/Publications/Basics/welfare/
Introduction.html

UMCOR Hunger/Poverty Ministries

http://gbgm-umc.org/units/UMCOR/hunger.html

UN ReliefWeb: Related Sites List

http://www.reliefweb.int/resource/related.html

part

2

U.S. Census Bureau: Poverty Areas

```
http://www.census.gov/pub/socdemo/www/povarea.html
```

U.S. DHHS: Federal Poverty Guidelines and Measurement

```
http://aspe.os.dhhs.gov/poverty/poverty.htm
```

Yahoo!: Welfare Reform

```
http://www.yahoo.com/Government/Politics/
Political_Issues/Welfare_Reform
```

Race and Ethnicity

Carnegie Mellon Race Links

```
http://eng.hss.cmu.edu/race
```

Cultural Survival

```
http://www.cs.org/
```

European Research Centre on Migration and Ethnic Relations

```
http://www.ercomer.org
```

Ethics Updates Page on Race, Multiculturalism and Ethnicity

```
http://ethics.acusd.edu/race.html
```

The Final Call: Black Community Issues and Events

```
http://www.finalcall.com
```

General Race & Ethnicity Resources—American Studies Web

```
http://www.georgetown.edu/crossroads/asw/
genethnic.html
```

Legal Information Institute: Civil Rights and Discrimination

```
http://fatty.law.cornell.edu/topics/civil_rights.html
```

National Civil Rights Museum

```
http://www.mecca.org/~crights/ncrm.html
```

Race and Ethnicity Online

http://www.providence.edu/polisci/rep/

Texas A&M Race and Ethnic Studies Institute

http://resi.tamu.edu/index.html

Trinity Sociology: Race and Ethnicity

http://WWW.Trinity.Edu/~mkearl/race.html

Voice of the Shuttle: Minority Studies Page

http://humanitas.ucsb.edu/shuttle/minority.html

WWW Virtual Library: Migration and Ethnic Relations

http://www.ercomer.org/wwwvl/

Yahoo!: Migration and Ethnic Relations

http://www.yahoo.com/Social_Science/
Migration_and_Ethnic_Relations

part

2

Yahoo!: Race Relations

http://dir.yahoo.com/Society_and_Culture/
Issues_and_Causes/Race_Relations/

Religion

American Academy of Religion

http://www.aar-site.org/

The Center for Reformed Theology and Apologetics

http://www.reformed.org/

Comparative Religion & Religious Studies

http://weber.u.washington.edu/~madin/

Cult Awareness & Information Centre—Australia

http://student.uq.edu.au/~py101663/zentry1.htm

Fighting the Radical Religious Right (useful links)

`http://ftp.qrd.org/qrd/www/rrr/rrrpage.html`

General Theory of Religion

`http://world.std.com/~awolpert`

Index of Religious Links

`http://www.religioustolerance.org/topicndx.htm`

Judaism and Jewish Resources

`http://shamash.org/trb/judaism.html`

New Religious Movements: Web Sites

`http://www.gtu.edu/library/LibraryNRMLinks.html`

part
2

Ontario Consultants on Religious Tolerance

`http://www.religioustolerance.org`

Religious Movements & Alternative Spirituality, An Annotated Directory of Internet Resources

`http://www.academicinfo.net/nrms.html`

Religious Resources on the Net

`http://www.aphids.com/relres/`

Religious Studies Electronic Library

`http://library.uwaterloo.ca/discipline/religious/`

Research Methods

ASA Section on Methods

`http://lion.icpsr.umich.edu/methsect`

Bill Trochim's Center for Social Research Methods

`http://trochim.human.cornell.edu/`

The Foundation Center (grants)

http://fdncenter.org

Glossary of Social Science Computing and Social Science Data Terms

http://odwin.ucsd.edu/glossary

Internet Research Journal

http://www.mcb.co.uk/cgi-bin/journal3/intr

PARnet: The Cornell Participatory Action Research Network

http://www.parnet.org

The Qualitative Report

http://www.nova.edu/ssss/QR/index.html

Research Engines for the Social Sciences

http://www.carleton.ca/~cmckie/research.html

Research Methods

http://www.siu.edu/~hawkes/methods.html

Research Resources for the Social Sciences

http://www.socsciresearch.com

Sociological Research Online

http://www.soc.surrey.ac.uk/socresonline

Statistics

Fedstats: One Stop Shopping for Federal Statistics

http://www.fedstats.gov/

SPSS Inc.

http://www.spss.com

part

2

Statistical Resources on the Web: Sociology

`http://www.lib.umich.edu/libhome/Documents.center/`
`stsoc.html`

Social Change

Data Center: A Resource for Progressive Social Change

`http://www.igc.org/datacenter/`

DOE's Center of Excellence for Sustainable Development

`http://www.sustainable.doe.gov`

Ed Brown's Resource Information: Global Change

`http://www.stile.lut.ac.uk/~gyedb/STILE/t0000459.html`

Good Works: A National Directory of Social Change Organizations

`http://www.essential.org/goodworks/`

Internet Resources on Sustainability

`http://www.chebucto.ns.ca/Environment/SCN/CommLink/`
`SCN-netguide.html`

Longwave and Social Cycles Resource Centre

`http://www.1-888.com/longwave/index.html`

Peace Brigades International

`http://www.igc.apc.org/pbi`

Peace Brigades International: Web Links

`http://www.igc.apc.org/pbi/links.html`

Social Change—A Collection of Relevant Book Chapters

`http://www.spc.uchicago.edu/ssr1/PRELIMS/change.html`

Soros Foundation Network for Open Society

http://www.soros.org

Talk 2000: Resources on the Bimillennial

http://humnet.humberc.on.ca/t2-res.htm

Social Psychology

ASA Social Psychology Section

http://www.asanet.org/sections/socpsych.html

Analyzing Social Interaction

http://www.msu.edu/user/amcconne/social.html

The British Journal of Social Psychology

http://journals.eecs.qub.ac.uk/BPS/BJSP/BJSP.html

Current Research in Social Psychology

http://www.uiowa.edu/~grpproc/crisp/crisp.html

George's Page (George Herbert Mead)

http://paradigm.soci.brocku.ca:80/~lward

Psychology Centre: Social and Cultural Psychology

http://server.bmod.athabascau.ca/html/aupr/social.htm

Social Psychology Network

http://www.socialpsychology.org/

Social Psychology Resources at Haverford College

http://www.haverford.edu/psych/SocPsycpage.html

Society for Personality and Social Psychology

http://spsp.clarion.edu/spsp/SPSP. HTM

part

2

A Sociological Social Psychology

http://www.trinity.edu/~mkearl/socpsy.html

SOSIG–World–Social Psychology

http://www.sosig.ac.uk/roads/subject-listing/World/
socpsyc.html

UWSP Psychology: Personality & Social Psychology Links

http://www.uwsp.edu/acad/psych/tpersoc.htm

Social Stratification

Albert Benschop's Alphabetical Bibliography on Class

http://www.pscw.uva.nl/sociosite/CLASS/bibA.html

International Stratification and Mobility File

http://fswinfo.fsw.ruu.nl/soc/HG/ismf

Stratification and Society

http://www.geocities.com/CollegePark/Quad/5889/
stratif.htm

What Is Social Stratification?

http://www.pitt.edu/~fvcst1/0010B-15.html

Social Structure and Social Interaction

Alliance for Redesigning Government

http://www.alliance.napawash.org/alliance/index.html

Core and Periphery in World Systems Analysis

http://www.stile.lut.ac.uk/~gyobs/GLOBAL/t0000095.html

Ed Brown's Political Economy Archive

http://www.stile.lut.ac.uk/~gyedb/STILE/index.html

Ed Brown's Resource Information: Capitalism

http://www.stile.lut.ac.uk/~gyedb/STILE/t0000460.html

Ed Brown's Resource Information: Development Theory

http://www.stile.lut.ac.uk/~gyedb/STILE/t0000425.html

Ed Brown's Resource Information; Neo-marxism

http://www.stile.lut.ac.uk/~gyedb/STILE/t0000455.html

A Gallery of Social Structures: Network Visualization

http://www.mpi-fg-koeln.mpg.de:80/~lk/netvis.html

Max Planck Institute for the Study of Societies

http://www.mpi-fg-koeln.mpg.de

WSN: The World-Systems Conferencing Electronic Network

http://csf.Colorado.EDU/wsystems

part
2

Sociological Theory

"An Outline of the Social System"

http://www.spc.uchicago.edu/ssr1/PRELIMS/Theory/
parsons.html

ASA Section on Marxist Sociology

http://csf.colorado.edu/psn/marxist-sociology/
index.html

Association for Humanist Sociology

http://www.kutztown.edu/~ehrensal/ahshome.html

The Common Theory Project

http://www.well.com/user/theory

Critical Theory-Driven Inquiry

http://www2.uchicago.edu/jnl-crit-inq

CTHEORY

http://www.ctheory.com/

The Marx/Engels Internet Archive

http://csf.Colorado.edu/psn/marx

Marx and Engels' Writings

http://english-www.hss.cmu.edu/marx

Norbert Elias and Process Sociology

http://www.usyd.edu.au/su/social/elias/elias.html

Political and Social Theory–Websites and Resources Directory

http://www.globalissues.net/Resources.
asp?CategoryName=Political+%26+Social+Theory

Postmodern Culture

http://jefferson.village.virginia.edu/pmc/
contents.all.html

Postmodern Thought Links at the University of Colorado, Denver

http://carbon.cudenver.edu/~mryder/itc_data/
postmodern.html

Society for the Study of Symbolic Interaction

http://sun.soci.niu.edu/~sssi

Sociology Links from Patrick Macartney

http://www.angelfire.com/ma/Socialworld/Sociology.html

Spoon Collective for Discussion of Philosophical Issues

http://jefferson.village.virginia.edu/~spoons

part

2

Tocqueville's Democracy in America

`http://xroads.virginia.edu/~HYPER/DETOC/home.html`

The Works of John Locke

`http://libertyonline.hypermall.com/Locke/Default.htm`

Technology and Computers

Alliance for Public Technology

`http://apt.org/index.html`

ASA Section on Sociology and Computers

`http://www.asanet.org/sections/computer.html`

Association for Computing Machinery

`http://www.acm.org/`

Association for Progressive Communications

`http://www.apc.org`

The Center for Democracy and Technology

`http://www.cdt.org/`

Center for the Study of Online Communities

`http://www.sscnet.ucla.edu/soc/csoc`

Computer Professionals for Social Responsibility

`http://www.cpsr.org/`

CTHEORY: Journal of Theory, Technology and Culture

`http://www.ctheory.com`

Scientists for Global Responsibility

`http://www.gn.apc.org/sgr`

Society for the Social Studies of Science

`http://www.lsu.edu:80/guests/ssss/public_html`

SPEED: Technology, Media, Society

`http://www.arts.ucsb.edu:80/~speed`

Street-Level Youth Media: Communications Technology for Youth

`http://www.iit.edu/~livewire`

 ## Violence and Abuse

BC Institute Against Family Violence

`http://www.bcifv.org/`

Child Abuse Links

`http://mail.med.upenn.edu/~jstoller/abuse.html`

ConflictNet: Conflict Resolution Resources

`http://www.igc.apc.org/conflictnet`

Domestic Violence Pages

`http://www.athens.net/~rblum/dvpindex.html`

Kate Orman's Violence Against Women Page

`http://www.ocs.mq.edu.au/~korman/feminism/vaw.html`

Links on Violence and Abuse, Q Web Sweden

`http://www.qweb.kvinnoforum.se/violence/index.html`

Links to Women's Resources from the El Paso Shelter for Battered Women

`http://www.utep.edu/departments/comm/students/
shelter/woman.html`

MINCAVA: Minnesota Center Against Violence and Abuse

`http://www.umn.edu`

National Network for Child Care: Child Abuse Links

`http://www.nncc.org/Abuse/abuse.links.html`

New York City Multidisciplinary Child Fatality Review

`http://www.sunlink.net/~browning/index.htm#home`

Nonviolence International

`http://www.igc.org/nonviolence/`

SafetyNet Domestic Violence Resources

`http://www.cybergrrl.com/dv.html`

Yahoo!: Domestic Violence Organizations

`http://www.yahoo.com/Society_and_Culture/Crime/Crimes/`
`Domestic_Violence/Organizations`

part

2

Documentation

Your Citation for Exemplary Research

There's another detail left for us to handle—the formal citing of electronic sources in academic papers. The very factor that makes research on the Internet exciting is the same factor that makes referencing these sources challenging: their dynamic nature. A journal article exists, either in print or on microfilm, virtually forever. A document on the Internet can come, go, and change without warning. Because the purpose of citing sources is to allow another scholar to retrace your argument, a good citation allows a reader to obtain information from your primary sources, to the extent possible. This means you need to include not only information on when a source was posted on the Internet (if available) but also when you obtained the information.

The two arbiters of form for academic and scholarly writing are the Modern Language Association (MLA) and the American Psychological Association (APA); both organizations have established styles for citing electronic publications.

MLA Style

In the fifth edition of the *MLA Handbook for Writers of Research Papers,* the MLA recommends the following formats:

- **URLs:** URLs are enclosed in angle brackets (<>) and contain the access mode identifier, the formal name for such indicators as "http" or "ftp." If a URL must be split across two lines, break it only after a slash (/). Never introduce a hyphen at the end of the first line. The URL should include all the parts necessary to identify uniquely the file/document being cited.

    `<http://www.csun.edu/~rtvfdept/home/index.html>`

- **An online scholarly project or reference database:** A complete online reference contains the title of the project or database (underlined); the name of the editor of the project or database (if given); electronic publication information, including version number (if relevant and if not part of the title), date of electronic publication or latest update, and name of any sponsoring institution or organization; date of access; and electronic address.

The Perseus Project. Ed. Gregory R. Crane.
    Mar. 1997. Dept. of Classics, Tufts U.
    15 June 1998 <http://www.perseus.tufts.edu/>.

If you cannot find some of the information, then include the information that is available. The MLA also recommends that you print or download electronic documents, freezing them in time for future reference.

- **A document within a scholarly project or reference database:** It is much more common to use only a portion of a scholarly project or database. To cite an essay, poem, or other short work, begin this citation with the name of the author and the title of the work (in quotation marks). Then include all the information used when citing a complete online scholarly project or reference database, however, make sure you use the URL of the specific work and not the address of the general site.

Cuthberg, Lori. "Moonwalk: Earthlings' Finest Hour."
    Discovery Channel Online. 1999. Discovery
    Channel. 25 Nov. 1999 <http://www.discovery.com/
    indep/newsfeatures/moonwalk/challenge.html>.

part **2**

■   **A professional or personal site:** Include the name of the person creating the site (reversed), followed by a period, the title of the site
(underlined), or, if there is no title, a description such as *Home page*
(such a description is neither placed in quotes nor underlined).
Specify the name of any school, organization, or other institution
affiliated with the site and follow it with your date of access and the
URL of the page.

```
Packer, Andy. Home page. 1 Apr. 1998
    <http://www.suu.edu/~students/Packer.htm>
```

Some electronic references are truly unique to the online domain.
These include email, newsgroup postings, MUDs (multiuser domains)
or MOOs (multiuser domains, object-oriented), and IRCs (Internet
Relay Chats).

Email   In citing email messages, begin with the writer's name (reversed) followed by a period, and the title of the message (if any) in quo-
tations as it appears in the subject line. Next comes a description of the
message, typically "Email to," and the recipient (e.g., "the author"), and
finally the date of the message.

```
Davis, Jeffrey. "Web Writing Resources." Email to
    Nora Davis. 3 Jan. 2000.

Sommers, Laurice. "Re: College Admissions Practices."
    Email to the author. 12 Aug. 1998.
```

List Servers and Newsgroups   In citing these references, begin with the
author's name (reversed) followed by a period. Next include the title of
the document (in quotes) from the subject line, followed by the words
"Online posting" (not in quotes). Follow this with the date of posting.
For list servers, include the date of access, the name of the list (if
known), and the online address of the list's moderator or administrator.
For newsgroups, follow "Online posting" with the date of posting, the
date of access, and the name of the newsgroup, prefixed with "news:"
and enclosed in angle brackets.

```
Applebaum, Dale. "Educational Variables." Online
    posting. 29 Jan. 1998. Higher Education
    Discussion Group. 30 Jan. 1993
    <jlucidoj@unc.edu>.
```

part

2

```
Gostl, Jack. "Re: Mr. Levitan." Online posting.
    13 June 1997. 20 June 1997
    <news:alt.edu.bronxscience>.
```

MUDs, MOOs, and IRCs   Begin with the name of the speaker(s) followed by a period. Follow with the description and date of the event, the forum in which the communication took place, the date of access, and the online address prefixed by "telnet://".

```
Guest. Personal interview. 13 Aug. 1998.
    <telnet://du.edu:8888>.
```

For more information on MLA documentation style, check out their Web site at http://www.mla.org/set_stl.htm

APA Style

The *Publication Manual of the American Psychological Association* (4th ed.) is fairly dated in its handling of online sources, having been published before the rise of the WWW and the generally recognized format for URLs. The format that follows is based on the APA manual, with modifications. It's important to remember that, unlike the MLA, the APA does not include temporary or transient sources (e.g., letters, phone calls, etc.) in its "References" page, preferring to handle them in in-text citations exclusively. This rule holds for electronic sources as well: email, MOOs/MUDs, list server postings, etc., are not included in the "References" page, merely cited in text, for example, "But Wilson has rescinded his earlier support for these policies" (Charles Wilson, personal email to the author, 20 November 1996). But also note that many list server and Usenet groups and MOOs actually archive their correspondences, so that there is a permanent site (usually a Gopher or FTP server) where those documents reside. In that case, you would want to find the archive and cite it as an unchanging source. Strictly speaking, according to the APA manual, a file from an FTP site should be referenced as follows:

```
Deutsch, P. (1991). Archie: An electronic directory
    service for the Internet [Online]. Available FTP:
    ftp.sura.net Directory: pub/archie/docs File:
    whatis.archie.
```

However, the increasing familiarity of Net users with the convention of a URL makes the prose description of how to find a file ("Avail-

able FTP: ftp.sura.net Directory: pub/archie/docs File: whatis.archie")
unnecessary.

So, modification of the APA format, (as suggested by the APA at its
Web site—www.apa.org), citations from the standard Internet sources
would appear as follows.

FTP (File Transfer Protocol) Sites To cite files available for downloading via FTP, give the author's name (if known), the publication date (if
available and if different from the date accessed), the full title of the
paper (capitalizing only the first word and proper nouns), the date of access, and the address of the FTP site along with the full path necessary
to access the file.

```
Deutsch, P. (1991) Archie: An electronic directory
     service for the Internet. Retrieved January 25,
     2000 from File Transfer Protocol: ftp://
     ftp.sura.net/pub/archie/docs/whatis.archie
```

WWW Sites (World Wide Web) To cite files available for viewing or
downloading via the World Wide Web, give the author's name (if
known), the year of publication (if known and if different from the date
accessed), the full title of the article, and the title of the complete work
(if applicable) in italics. Include any additional information (such as versions, editions, or revisions) in parentheses immediately following the
title. Include the date of retrieval and the full URL (the http address).

```
Burka, L. P. (1993). A hypertext history of multi-
     user dungeons. MUDdex. Retrieved January 13, 1997
     from the World Wide Web: http://www.utopia.com/
     talent/lpb/muddex/essay/

Tilton, J. (1995). Composing good HTML (Vers. 2.0.6).
     Retrieved December 1, 1996 from the World Wide Web:
     http://www.cs.cmu.edu/~tilt/cgh/
```

Synchronous Communications (MOOs, MUDs, IRC, etc.) Give the name of
the speaker(s), the complete date of the conversation being referenced in
parentheses, and the title of the session (if applicable). Next, list the title
of the site in italics, the protocol and address (if applicable), and any directions necessary to access the work. Last, list the date of access, followed by the retrieval information. Personal interviews do not need to
be listed in the References, but do need to be included in parenthetic references in the text (see the APA *Publication Manual*).

part

2

```
Cross, J. (1996, February 27). Netoric's Tuesday
    cafe: Why use MUDs in the writing classroom?
    MediaMoo. Retrieved March 1, 1996 from File
    Transfer Protocol: ftp://daedalus.com/
    pub/ACW/NETORIC/catalog
```

Gopher Sites List the author's name (if applicable), the year of publication, the title of the file or paper, and the title of the complete work (if applicable). Include any print publication information (if available) followed by the protocol (i.e., gopher://). List the date that the file was accessed and the path necessary to access the file.

```
Massachusetts Higher Education Coordinating
    Council. (1994). Using coordination
    and collaboration to address change. Retrieved
    July 16, 1999 from the World Wide Web:
    gopher://gopher.mass.edu:170/00gopher_root%3A%5B_
    hecc%5D_plan
```

Email, Listservs, and Newsgroups Do not include personal email in the list of References. Although unretrievable communication such as email is not included in APA References, somewhat more public or accessible Internet postings from newsgroups or listservs may be included. See the APA *Publication Manual* for information on in-text citations.

```
Heilke, J. (1996, May 3). Webfolios. Alliance for
    Computers and Writing Discussion List. Retrieved
    December 31, 1996 from the World Wide Web:
    http://www.ttu.edu/lists/acw-1/9605/0040.html
```

Other authors and educators have proposed similar extensions to the APA style, too. You can find URLs to these pages at

`www.psychwww.com/resource/apacrib.htm`

Another frequently-referenced set of extensions is available at

`www.uvm.edu/~ncrane/estyles/apa.htm`

Remember, "frequently-referenced" does not equate to "correct" or even "desirable." Check with your professor to see if your course or school has a preference for an extended APA style.

Glossary

Your Own Private Glossary

The Glossary in this book contains reference terms you'll find useful as you get started on the Internet. After a while, however, you'll find yourself running across abbreviations, acronyms, and buzzwords whose definitions will make more sense to you once you're no longer a novice (or "newbie"). That's the time to build a glossary of your own. For now, the 2DNet Webopædia gives you a place to start.

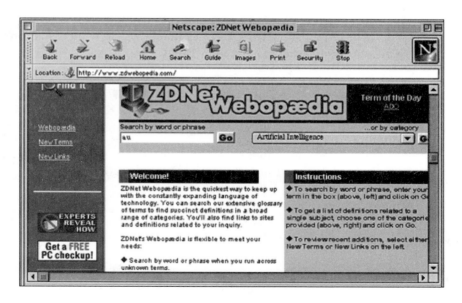

alias
A simple email address that can be used in place of a more complex one.

AVI
Audio Video Interleave. A video compression standard developed for use with Microsoft Windows. Video clips on the World Wide Web are usually available in both AVI and QuickTime formats.

bandwidth
Internet parlance for capacity to carry or transfer information such as email and Web pages.

BBS
Bulletin Board System. A dial-up computer service that allows users to post messages and download files. Some BBSs are connected to and provide access to the Internet, but many are self-contained.

browser
The computer program that lets you view the contents of Web sites.

client
A program that runs on your personal computer and supplies you with Internet services, such as getting your mail.

cyberspace
The whole universe of information that is available from computer networks. The term was coined by science fiction writer William Gibson in his novel *Neuromancer,* published in 1984.

DNS
See **domain name server.**

domain
A group of computers administered as a single unit, typically belonging to a single organization such as a university or corporation.

domain name
A name that identifies one or more computers belonging to a single domain. For example, "apple.com".

domain name server
A computer that converts domain names into the numeric addresses used on the Internet.

download
Copying a file from another computer to your computer over the Internet.

email
Electronic mail.

emoticon
A guide to the writer's feelings, represented by typed characters, such as the Smiley :-). Helps readers understand the emotions underlying a written message.

FAQ
Frequently Asked Questions

flame
A rude or derogatory message directed as a personal attack against an individual or group.

flame war
An exchange of flames (see above).

FTP
File Transfer Protocol, a method of moving files from one computer to another over the Internet.

home page
A page on the World Wide Web that acts as a starting point for information about a person or organization.

hypertext
Text that contains embedded *links* to other pages of text. Hypertext enables the reader to navigate between pages of related information by following links in the text.

LAN:
Local Area Network. A computer network that is located in a concentrated area, such as offices within a building.

link
A reference to a location on the Web that is embedded in the text of the Web page. Links are usually highlighted with a different color or underline to make them easily visible.

list server
Strictly speaking, a computer program that administers electronic mailing lists, but also used to denote such lists or discussion groups, as in "the writer's list server."

lurker
A passive reader of an Internet *newsgroup*. A lurker reads messages, but does not participate in the discussion by posting or responding to messages.

mailing list
A subject-specific automated e-mail system. Users subscribe and receive e-mail from other users about the subject of the list.

modem
A device for connecting two computers over a telephone line.

newbie
A new user of the Internet.

newsgroup
A discussion forum in which all participants can read all messages and public replies between the participants.

pages
All the text, graphics, pictures, and so forth, denoted by a single URL beginning with the identifier "http://".

plug-in
A third-party software program that will lend a web browser (Netscape, Internet Explorer, etc.) additional features.

quoted
Text in an email message or newsgroup posting that has been set off by the use of vertical bars or > characters in the left-hand margin.

search engine
A computer program that will locate Web sites or files based on specified criteria.

secure
A Web page whose contents are encrypted when sending or receiving information.

server
A computer program that moves information on request, such as a Web server that sends pages to your browser.

Smiley
See **emoticon.**

snail mail
Mail sent the old fashioned way: Write a letter, put it in an envelope, stick on a stamp, and drop it in the mailbox.

spam
Spam is to the Internet as unsolicited junk mail is to the postal system.

URL
Uniform Resource Locator: The notation for specifying addresses on the World Wide Web (e.g. http://www.abacon.com or ftp://ftp.abacon.com).

Usenet
The section of the Internet devoted to *newsgroups.*

Web browser
A program used to navigate and access information on the World Wide Web. Web browsers convert html coding into a display of pictures, sound, and words.

Web site
A collection of World Wide Web pages, usually consisting of a home page and several other linked pages.